BEAUTIFUL SPIRITS

A Medium's Gifts Return

by
J. B. Duncan

Copyright © 2018 by J B Duncan & Christine K. Duncan
All Rights Reserved. No part of this publication may be reproduced, distributed, or transmitted in any form or by any means, including photocopy, recording, or other electronic or mechanical methods, without the prior written permission of the author.
For permission requests or enquiries, please email the author at christinekyrin@gmail.com

First published 2018 Sweetfields Publishing House
Wingham 2429
N.S.W. Australia

Edited by Moonlit Magic Creations.
Cover, Interior Graphics/Art Credit: Christine K. Duncan
Pictures on pages 4, 33, 65, 88, 182 and all flying dove pictures, all sourced from Internet copyright-free images. The image on page 130, titled "Red deer, Bradgate Park" is copyright to Julian Dowse, and licenced for reuse here: sourced from geograph.org.uk - 992321.jpg
Note: Julian Dowse does not endorse the author of this book or its contents.

Because of the dynamic nature of the Internet, any web addresses or links contained in this book may have changed since publication and may no longer be valid. The views expressed in this work are solely those of the author and do not necessarily reflect the views of the publisher, and the publisher hereby disclaims any responsibility for them.

The author of this book does not dispense medical advice or prescribe the use of any technique as a form of treatment for physical, emotional, or medical problems without the advice of a physician, either directly or indirectly. The intent of the author is only to offer information of a general nature to help you in your quest for emotional and spiritual wellbeing.

In the event you use any of the information in this book for yourself, the author and the publisher assume no responsibility for your actions.

This book contains the names of people of actual events. In almost all instances permission to reproduce their names has been granted by the person, or persons, involved. In some instances, said person(s) have chosen to be given an alias. For those stories for which permission has not been gained, and where names may be used, the application of an alias also appears.

Acknowledgements

For all of those people who have read my first book, *My Encounters with the Spirit World*, I thank you. I hope you enjoyed it and, most of all, that you were able to identify with, or be comforted by, any of the stories contained within it: all were true accounts from my years of experience as a medium and psychic in the 1970's to the turn of the century.

You have no doubt had 'strange' or psychic experiences yourself, or perhaps you have recognised similar spiritual encounters through your friends', relatives', or close family members' stories. Many readers have told me how they enjoyed this book and how a spirit loved-one has come to them, if merely to let them know they were there.

My Encounters with the Spirit World was written and designed according to what Spirit directed. It might be mine in name but it is otherwise Spirit's book. Late in 2012 I was told I would be writing a second book, this one about the return of my Gifts and, surprisingly, of gaining new Gifts. I decided to include some stories of people who have also had spiritual encounters.

So *Beautiful Spirits*, on the other hand, is mine – with Spirit's help. I chose the stories with my clients' permissions and also the design of the book's cover, as well as its title. Again, I was very fortunate to have my daughter's help in the entire process of putting it all together. I would be lost without her, so a very big "thank you" to Christine.

In almost all cases, I have kindly been granted permission from my clients, as well as from those who have contributed their first-hand accounts, for inclusion in this book. A few of these people have preferred to use an alias instead of their real name. But sometimes there were occasions where I wasn't able to ask the person for their permission, as their story may have happened quite a while ago, or they have since died, so I have also used alias for them as well.

I trust you will find *Beautiful Spirits* just as intriguing, enjoyable and informative as my first book.

Regards,
Joyce

CONTENTS

Arthur   1
Arthur's life of Tragedies   12

PART ONE: Beautiful Spirits

Australia Day at the Markets	24
Lydia, my Beautiful Angel	29
My New Zealand Cousin	35
The Mischievous Child	39
Tina's Visit	52
The Lost Girl	58
The Coloured 'Hearse'	64
Rob's Dad	67
The Friends I've Had to Farewell	74
"Mike" not "Mark"	79
Guided by my Beautiful Late Son	81
Strange Coincidences	84
Elsie	87
The WWI Soldier	95
Pictures Can Tell a Thousand Words	98
The Mother in the Wheelchair	104
The Broadmeadow Exhibition	109
"Mum's Here"	115
The Spirit of a Living Baby	119
An Interesting Telephone Call	124
Another Market	128
Kym	133
The Young Man and the Cemetery	137

CONTENTS

PART TWO: Animal, Dreams and Visions

Two Best Mates	142
The Lady Who had been a Horse	145
The Spirit Stag	147
Sasha's Visit	150
The Scared Collie Dog	155
Kitten by the Curtain	157
The Dogs are Okay	158
The 'Boarding' House	161
Julie and the Jockey	163
Kissed by the Angel of Death	170
A Family Reunion… of sorts	180
My Vision of Madeline	184

PART THREE: True Ghost Stories

A Heavenly Encounter	195
Belinda's Brush with a Bad Entity	198
Nanna and Her Simpatcona	202
Michelle's Nanna	205
The Feather at the Footy	209
Meet Me at the Races	213
Bobbie's Bookmark	220
A Meditation into the Spirit World	226

Picture Credits

Arthur as the Groom's Best Man* 22

Cousin Gerry* 38

Sissy's Signed Book 50
Courtesy Sissy

Tina* 57

Quarantine Station 63
Courtesy Internet-free source

Elsie 94
Supplied by M. Janes

Red Roses 97
Courtesy Vestaka, Deviantart

Couple with Vegetable Stall* 102

Janelle's Dad & Mum 106
Courtesy J. Smith

'Spirit' Stag 149
Credit Julian Dowse

Sasha 154
Credit C. K. Duncan

Mum, Hilda & Tess* 156

Sandy* 160

Jesus Figurine* 199

Nanna Janes 208
Supplied by M. Janes

Dad, Robert 212

Car Racetrack 219
Supplied by Dave

Bookmark* 225

* *Courtesy J. B. Duncan*

Arthur

Editor's NOTE: The following contains graphic description of an actual event, see ✦ (page 5)

My life stopped briefly when, in 1997, I lost my beautiful son and first-born child, Arthur. On Saturday the 6th of September he'd turned thirty-five. This was also the day Princess Diana was laid to rest. Her death – which was one week earlier and coincided with my birthday on August 31st – struck him hard.

He was devastated by her death and like many people, he adored her and found it very difficult to come to terms with the way in which she'd died. Her passing and funeral threw him into a spin as he watched its coverage on the television, and we could see he was terribly saddened by the whole experience.

We were lucky to have had this wonderful child; he had a lovely personality, very placid and gentle. He would give you the shirt off his back if you were cold and give you his last coin if you were short of cash. Sadly, he had no girlfriend, was never married nor had any children. He did, however, fall deeply in love with a young woman at his workplace, located on the Central Coast of New South Wales, eastern Australia.

Considering Arthur was a shy person since his childhood and lacked sufficient confidence in his adult years – particularly when he wanted to get to know a girl – he had fought hard to make a respectable impression on her. She had all the qualities he was looking for in a partner and was perhaps the first woman he really cared to call a girlfriend.

There were days when he struggled to get up for work, but it was because of her that he persevered. *She* was the reason he put up with the early starts, the half-hour travel to his job, the long hours it demanded and, the frequent teasing and bullying he received from his work colleagues. Apparently, she had encouraged his early attentions in the way she dressed, smiled or looked at him, which continued right up until the day he was fired.

Eventually he mustered up the courage to ask her out, though she turned him down. He tried a few more times over the following months, to no avail and one day, when he was in a particularly good mood, he decided to ask her out just, "in case she'd changed her mind," he'd said. Sadly, her response was, "I'm not interested in anyone, especially you. And I think you're a jerk and your weird!"

This crushed his heart and made him feel terribly bad. She then went to the manager and said Arthur had been harassing her for too long. Immediately following this, he was called to the manager's office and told he had to pack up his things at the end of the day's work and leave. He was fired, simple as that. When he arrived home that afternoon, his face was as white as a sheet, horrified things could have gone so badly. I still remember him walking in the door…

"Hi Mum," he murmured, as if in another world.

"Hi… what's up?" I said, instantly worried.

"I've just been fired…" he said quietly.

"Fired? Why?" I said with a fluster,

"Because Denise just told the boss I was harassing her, and the boss called me to the office and said, "At the end of the day I want you to pack up your things and don't bother coming back, because you're fired!". But I didn't think I'd done anything wrong!"

I gave my son a big hug, said how sorry I was to hear it, then Arthur went into his room and I didn't see him for a while after that. He came out and had dinner then, murmuring, "Good night", he went straight back to bed.

The next day he arose early for breakfast and was cleaned and dressed as though ready to leave the house. Arthur always took care in his appearance and made sure his hair was nicely combed, his clothes tidy and his personal hygiene in order. He was brought up with 'old school' values so he would have also enjoyed looking after his 'lady', such as opening and closing the door for her, taking her out for a nice meal or movie and buying her little gifts he thought she'd find pleasing.

"What's up? Where are you going?" I asked, surprised he was even out of bed.

"I've got to go to town, and I will call in and see Denise and apologise," he said, clearly troubled.

"I wouldn't if I were you," I gently warned. "Let it be. She's not worth it."

As it turned out, Denise didn't want to see him. Apparently she'd refused to talk to him in person; somebody took his message to her instead. He came home disappointed, only to explain the awful treatment they'd also given him while there.

Approximately six weeks later he called in again to this workplace to see her, having caught her during her lunch break.

She'd said, "If you don't leave me alone I'll get my friends to take care of you!"

She went on to say, "Just leave me alone, I don't want to talk to you!"

All he wanted to do was apologise – he didn't mean to upset her or cause her any harm.

"Bugger off!" she'd snapped, "Or I'll get my 'friends' to come after you and they will hurt you!"

"I don't know why," he said to me when relaying the encounter. "I wasn't doing any harm. I just wanted to apologise…"

"Don't worry about it," I replied, wanting to sooth him. "You're better off without her. Try and forget her."

"The trouble is, I can't. She's beautiful!"

For a while he floundered, for at his age, it seemed, he couldn't get another job and as a result, he just got more depressed. About three months after being fired, I noticed his attitude change slightly; he became very hermit-like, he was very depressed with life and couldn't sit still for long. Even when watching T.V. he was up and down every half hour or so. I could see him slowly turning into himself for answers as to why she was so nasty to him, when all he wanted was her friendship.

At the end of July came the news that had devastated Australia: a huge landslide at Thredbo, in the Snowy Mountains country of New South Wales, killed eighteen people, among them, the wife of sole survivor, Stuart Diver. The news affected Arthur badly, and then, less than a month later, we heard of Mother Teresa's death. Right behind that, of course, was Princess Diana's fatal car crash.

Like many people, Arthur adored her, and his depression sunk lower than ever in the days following this tragic event. Her funeral must have been one of the saddest things for him. In Australia, the next day was Sunday – Father's Day.

My second-born child, and eldest daughter, Debbie, lived next door to us in those days and she came over this particular afternoon with a little cake to celebrate his birthday and Clive's Father's Day. The mood was quiet and terribly gloomy but we made the most of it to cheer him up.

At eleven o'clock that night, Debbie left us to go back to her home, and Clive and I said goodnight to Arthur, as was our custom. I gave him a kiss on the cheek and a big hug, telling him everything would be "alright tomorrow". I went to bed hoping he would feel better in the morning. But it wasn't to be.

This would be the last time I would hug my son.

Clive went into a deep sleep soon after retiring. Two hours later, after worrying about Arthur and trying to fall asleep, thinking he was in his bed, I finally fell asleep too.

And then I heard it… the noise of a very loud horn, blowing in the still of the night.

I looked at the clock; it was one-thirty-five a.m. I realised it was the last train coming up from Sydney on its way north. We lived right across the road from the main train line that links this city to all the coastal towns south of the Queensland border. But why was it blasting its horn?

It got louder and louder the closer it came to us, having started at perhaps six hundred meters away, continuing as the train passed through the level train crossing just down from the house, and more insistent with every second. The train's wheels screeched in the night air, the metal actually grinding under the pressure to stop too quickly. The sounds were curdling – like water being poured down the funnel of a large horn – a distinct noise that I'll never forget; it haunts me still. It seemed to go on forever. I thought it would never stop and would wake up the neighbourhood.

Then it happened, literally right opposite our home…
THUMP!
My husband woke up screaming.
"Oh my god! He's hit something, or someone!"

I tried to reassure him that everything would be alright, but he wouldn't settle. So I suggested we get dressed and go over to check it out. This would be an awful mistake.

By the time I was dressed Clive had already bolted out the front door, in his pyjamas, and across the road to the fence that was supposed to rail off public access to the line.

As I finally approached the front gate of our driveway, Clive stumbled in, his face as white as a sheet, crying, "It's Arthur! It's Arthur! The train hit Arthur!"

"Don't be silly! Arthur's in bed!" I replied and, looking towards Arthur's bedroom, I added, "See? His light is still on!"

"It's Arthur I tell you! I saw him!"

Clive was now starting to hold his right arm and his breathing was rushed. I helped him inside the house to the lounge and made him sit. Then, quietly praying, I walked to my son's room, hoping all the time that I would see him in his bed. But it was not to be. As I opened his door I felt a strong, backwards pull, as though someone was trying to warn me of my biggest disappointment to come.

The first thing I saw there was some envelopes with messages in them, named and left to us from him. As for Arthur, he was nowhere to be seen. I went cold. The pull, I think, may have been his spirit trying to hold me back, perhaps to avoid any pain I may have felt. This, of course, would be inevitable.

Trembling, I now wanted to see for myself if it really was him on the train line, so I made my way back to the front door. But then I saw Clive lying on the lounge, clutching at his chest.

"What's up?" I asked, torn between the two.

"I'm having a heart attack!" he croaked.

I panicked. "What can I do?"

"I've rung the ambulance. They're on their way here!" he said, fighting back the tears.

Numb with shock, I turned for the door.

"Don't go over there," Clive begged.

"But I've got to! I have to prove to myself that it's not Arthur the train has hit!"

"But it *is* him! I've already told you that! You don't need to see it!"

I was desperate.

"How do you know he hasn't gone for a walk and will be back home shortly?"

"Because he didn't…"

But I didn't listen. I didn't want to stand around arguing about it. My son, my beautiful, sweet, gentle-natured boy could not have done something so stupid, so… so utterly awful. I left the house, trusting the ambulance would turn up at any minute. I rushed next door to let my daughter, Debbie, know what had just happened. I banged on her front door, screaming her name and woke her up. After explaining the situation to her, I told her to go and look after her father, then I crossed the road. Something told me to brace myself for the worst thing in my life I would ever see, for the outcome was going to be very hard to swallow...

The area beyond the fence was very dark. I noticed a flashlight in the distance coming from behind the rear-end of the train.

"Hello, can you hear me?" I called out, "Did the train hit a young man with a beard?"

The voice replying to me was understandably guarded.

"Why do you want to know?" he said.

"Because my son is not in his room and I am worried it may be him!" I said.

"Go up to the front of the train and tell the constable in charge what you have just told me!" he replied with care.

"Thank you!" I said and immediately hurried up the road to where the front of the train stood.

Police were milling around now and I asked one of them to let me speak with the constable in charge. While waiting for him, I kept looking down the line and I noticed a lot of railway men running around, gathering up bits and pieces off the tracks. I dreaded that that was my son's remains. I wanted the constable to hurry up and talk with me, I was so nervous and anxious, and all the while my husband needed emergency care. Just as I was about to ask someone if the constable was coming, he appeared.

"What's your problem, Madam? How can I help you?" he asked, not unkindly.

"I was wondering what, or who, the train had hit please," I replied, trying to hold it together.

He looked puzzled at me.

"Why do you want to know?" he queried. "Why is it so important to you?"

"Well, my husband and I heard the train hit something, or someone, and he raced over to the fence to see what it was. He reckons he saw our son's head just lying there. But I'm not convinced. And my son is not in his bedroom!"

The constable was calm in his reply.

"What does your son look like? And where do you live?" he asked.

"I live over there where the light is on," I began, pointing down the road, "and my son is thirty-five years old, with short black, curly hair and he has a reddish beard. My husband is in shock and is also having a heart attack. I need an ambulance for him." I must have sounded as if I was babbling, but I too, was in shock.

"I would like you to go home to your husband," he calmly said, "and as soon as we can I will send you the ambulance from here to your place. Then I'll come and see you when I know more."

I returned home within minutes, to find Clive gasping for air.

"The policeman is sending his ambulance as soon as he can," I said, wanting to reassure him. Before I could say another word, an ambulance arrived, quickly followed by a second. When they were satisfied that we only needed the one, the second ambulance left.

The crew worked quickly to stabilise Clive; they checked his pulse, his eyes, his heart, even his breathing, until they were convinced they were dealing with a genuine heart attack. The time seemed to drag on, but it was only ten minutes from when they had arrived to when I heard that fatal knock on my front door.

I froze, knowing intuitively that it was the police, and just as the ambulance crew were preparing to take my husband to the hospital, too! I dreaded answering the door. I was still hoping I would prove Clive wrong and that the constable would say something like, "You don't need to worry yourself. It was not your son, but it was another young man that resembled your son's description. Maybe your son went for a walk". That would have been really good news but no, instead came…

"Hello!" The man's face was straight, neither smiling nor sad. "Can you tell me if your son wore a white Terry Towelling dressing gown please?"

I knew then that I was in for some bad news, for Arthur's favourite dressing gown was exactly that.

"Yes," I answered. "Don't tell me it was him!"

"I am afraid it was," he said.

I invited him in to see my husband's condition.

At this point I was suddenly feeling very calm, and warm, as though someone was giving me a big hug. I assumed it was Arthur, my beautiful first-born, reassuring me that he was now at peace and no longer in any miserable pain. I also sensed spiritual family members around Clive, giving him their love and support in his need, trying to comfort him as best they could do. Even though I couldn't see them as I once had, I could feel their presence around us.

When the constable realised that Clive was suitably looked after, he asked to see Arthur's room. I took him to the door and allowed him to go in. The first thing that he saw, of course, was a tidy appearance, with the letters neatly laid out on the bed. He asked me for some information about my son's behaviour leading up to this dreadful night. I told him about his depression and what I thought may have caused it. He finished looking around the room and then we went back in to the lounge room.

"I think it would be a good idea for you to go with your husband to the hospital," he said to me.

I pondered on this, worrying for our two little Maltese dogs, who were caught up in the stress and rush of the experience. They were relatively young and I really didn't care to leave them locked up in the house alone.

"I'd prefer to stay home with the little ones," I said anxiously.

"You're better off coming to the hospital with your husband, in case he needs you," a paramedic said.

I sort of came to realise that they didn't want me staying home by myself, but at the time I didn't understand why. Reluctantly I locked up the house and put newspaper down for the pups and then left with the policeman.

It wasn't until the next morning, just as the sun was rising, when the constable came to the hospital to see how we were doing.

I told him that I was upset at leaving our little ones at home when I knew Clive would be in good hands with the hospital staff. This is when he told me the reason why they'd insisted I come to the hospital with him: they were worried I would have gone over to the railway line after the paramedics had left the house. What I would have seen would scar me for life – as my beloved husband is scarred. What they didn't realise was that, out of respect for Arthur, I wouldn't have gone over there.

I accepted his reasoning anyway and asked if we could go home to 'the kids', and to get Clive some breakfast and start making the rounds of those awful phone calls to the relatives. Of course, it was up to the doctor treating him to give the all-clear and around two hours later, we were allowed to leave, so long as Clive rested and took things steadily. I arranged with Debbie to come and pick us up, and soon enough we were back home with our two beautiful 'puppies', who were very excited to see us. Best of all, neither of them had messed anywhere on the floor, but had held on until being let out to the garden.

There is more of this story in *My Encounters with the Spirit World*, which you will find in the chapter, *Farewell My Son*.

It has now been over twenty years since Arthur passed on and we all miss him still, but I also know, deep in my heart, that he is far happier, far healthier than he ever was in this life.

Thank you, Arthur, for being our beloved son.

൞ඏ

Arthur's Life of Tragedies

Sadly, Arthur's life started with trauma right from his birth. Unfortunately there was a few occasions in which he'd died. Now I didn't know of them all – three of course, I did. But it was in the midst of December 2017 when my lovely son came to me (from spirit), to tell me of them all.

He said, "Mum, I would like you to write it down what happened to me. I want you to tell the people about all of the times that I had died."

"All of the times?" I had asked. "But you only died twice, and the third time was the last one in which you didn't come back!"

"No," he said, "I died a total of five times in all. But you weren't told about the other two. And no one else knows about most of them anyway. That's why I want you to write it down and to put it in your book. They should know. I want them to know, and don't worry about missing out anything because I'll help you," he reassured.

And this is what he told me, in his words…

"In my second week after I was born, I got sick. I didn't have normal bowel movements and my nappy was mostly dry. By the third week I couldn't keep any food down. Within minutes of you [Mum] feeding me, I would throw up all over you."

I remembered this time well enough – he tried to drink my milk but couldn't, bringing it back as he'd said. Soon enough his vomiting was so quick, so instant, that it would fly across the room like spray from a spray can. I didn't know what to do; I was a new mum with a troubled baby. I talked to my family doctor about him, hoping he'd be able to help the little mite get well again, but all he said was, "If it doesn't settle down by the end of the week we'll send you to see the specialist."

Well, it didn't. By his fourth week I was admitted to the women's hospital, called, "The Tresillian", a place for mums with sick babies, where the two of us would be watched over by trained doctors and nurses, who observed our behaviours. After a week of this he was suddenly taken to Camperdown Children's Hospital, needing an urgent operation. I didn't know this had happened until a doctor came to me and told me what was going on.

The doctor here explained what Arthur's situation was and what he was going to do for him to fix the situation, using diagrams and terms that I could hardly follow. At six weeks old, Arthur had finally been diagnosed with *Plyoric Stenosis*.

This is where a valve leading to the digestive system allows food to enter into the stomach, like a door which opens when food is present and closes when there's nothing to be digested. But for Arthur, his valve closed when food was waiting to go in, causing a build-up that, naturally, had nowhere to go but back up through his mouth. So that afternoon, he was rushed to Camperdown for a nine o'clock operation that night.

Clive and I arrived there by seven p.m. and thankfully, we were allowed to see him before he was taken in for the operation. In his room, our little baby lay motionless, with tubes coming out from his nose and mouth, his skin white as a sheet. It scared us dreadfully, for he looked dead and for a horrible heartbeat, I believed it was so. But then I noticed his breathing, which was shallow, so I knew he was surviving… just.

At around eight p.m. we were ushered into a waiting room, feeling anxious and upset, while the nursing staff prepared Arthur for his operation. Time seemed to drag on, when we noticed that it was now coming up to eleven p.m. Finally an intern came to see us with some good news…

And some bad, too.

"Your son is okay," he said in a calm voice. "The doctor is with him now. We've had to put him on hold as we've had another emergency come in."

Arthur had still not been operated on; Clive and I feared the worst.

"Don't panic yet!" the intern went on. "Your son is up next and we'll be operating on him at eleven-forty-five."

Naturally, we wanted to argue, to say something in return that could justify our dismay, though we didn't.

"He's okay," the intern repeated, trying to keep us calm, "but it'll be a little longer than we expected, and we'll let you know when it's all over. Just relax and go have a cup of tea."

Our hearts sank very low – would everything really be okay?

As it turned out, Arthur would recover, but he would not be the same again. It was around midnight when the doctor, who did the operation, came into the waiting room with a smile on his face.

"The operation went well and everything is fine," he said gently. "Your son is out of danger now, but if we had waited another fifteen minutes, it would have been too late, for he would have died."

It was terrible news to hear. But that wasn't the worst of it, not for me, now, for as this bit of history played out in my memory, Arthur's spirit gave me the truth of the actual situation back then.

> "That's not true, Mum," he said very earnestly.
> "I did die. The doctor didn't tell you the whole story. He didn't want you and Dad to get upset.

> They were about to operate on me when I stopped breathing for a few minutes. That's when they realised they had to work quickly to get me back. It was very tense for everyone at the time. But as you can see, I did fight it, and pulled through for you and Dad."

It was a rather annoying thing to learn, this many years later, that my beautiful boy – who'd struggled in the first start of his life – really *had* died on that occasion. It was very heartbreaking to hear these words, it hurt me deeply knowing I had been lied to, his own mother. Yet it was also important to have heard it from Arthur himself, and for that I am grateful.

ಹಂಡ

Well the months passed and around August 1964, when he was almost into his second birthday, he got the dreaded Whooping Cough. We had only been in our new home for about three months. His coughing was so bad for most of the night that we brought him into our bed, hoping to sooth him. I was crying to see his face so red, and knowing he was in such distress. We were frantic that he wouldn't make it to the morning, when the doctor's surgery would be open; in those days we only had an after-hours service number to call, otherwise it was an emergency case with an ambulance to hospital.

By six-forty-five a.m. we realised we had to make that call, for Arthur was now very much in worse condition. Clive explained Arthur's situation to the telephone operator and fifteen minutes later, our doctor arrived – right on seven o'clock.

Our boy was lying on our bed, his lips now turning blue; he had stopped breathing AGAIN!

"The doctor's just pulled up out the front! Tell him Arthur's stopped breathing! Hurry!" I screamed to Clive.

Next thing I know, the doctor rushed into our room with his bag, took out a syringe and put it in Arthur's arm. Within minutes our son took a deep breath.

The doctor was relieved, of course, as he'd arrived just in time. Arthur's recovery was slow, yet promising. We, too, felt a deep relief. We were given medication for our son to take every four hours until he returned to normal.

This was the first time Arthur had died that I knew of and reliving it for this book has been hard, but perhaps healing, too. The next time was simply horrific.

༺༻

At age three-and-a-half it happened again. It was Mother's Day 1965. We were now living in our new house and my parents had come to visit us. I had my thirteen-month-old daughter, Debbie, with us, too. Clive was out in the front yard, working on a retaining wall when he decided to go to the nearest quarry for some sandstone blocks. David, my Dad, offered to go with him to help load the trailer, but neither he nor Clive had had experience in turning and reversing box trailers.

Clive has always been a safe driver and he had decided to utilise the new neighbour's unused driveway opposite our own to park the car and trailer, where they would then unhook the trailer, reverse the car back onto the road, turn the trailer around and re-hook it afterwards. At that same time, another neighbour, Basil, who lived two doors down and also across the road from us, was driving home from church. Unawares to any of us, Arthur had seen his Dad and Pop busy with the car out in the street and he'd decided to go after him.

Arthur idolised Clive, wanting to be with him wherever he went. So while the adults were preoccupied with the car and trailer, and with Basil driving down the road to his own home, young Arthur ran up our driveway to be with his Dad. No one saw the toddler run onto the road.

Thank goodness Basil was only going slowly, for suddenly his car went over the top of my boy. Clive turned in time to see him rolling under the car, thinking he was only a cardboard box. But Basil stopped to find out what he'd hit (for he didn't know it was Arthur, either). That's when Clive saw his son, lying motionless, on the ground at the back of the car. He didn't hesitate.

Instead, clutching our son's body, he'd jumped into Basil's car, shouting, "Take us to the hospital, please! It's Arthur! You've hit my son!"

Basil raced them off – Clive and our baby – eager to get them emergency care.

Dad, meanwhile, was speechless with shock and Mum and I, busy indoors, had no idea what had just happened. The next we knew, Dad came bursting into the house, out of breath.

"Quick you've got to come with me to the hospital now!" he cried, looking stricken. "Arthur's just been run over!"

I struggled to catch up.

"What, How?" I asked. "He was just here a couple of moments ago! How could this happen so quickly?"

Dad explained the situation and offered to drive me to the hospital, while Mum stayed to look after Debbie, and our house.

Dad dropped me off at the hospital, shaking with nerves, saying, "When you are ready to come on home, ring me and I'll come back and pick you up."

"Okay," I replied, and hurried off to the emergency entrance.

Later that night we rang home and told Dad we were ready to leave, and that we were bringing Arthur home with us. We arrived around eight p.m. and carefully bundled our boy into his bed. He was heavily bandaged around his head. Clive decided to sleep next to him in case Arthur woke up through the night, there to comfort him should he need it.

I had asked him if Arthur had died on the way to hospital.

"No," he'd replied.

As this memory played out in my mind all these years later, this is when spirit-Arthur again intervened.

"Yes Mum, I did. But Dad was in too much shock to notice," he said. "I actually died briefly in the car and again in the hospital. But again, I fought it and survived."

He *was* lucky again, no doubt about it. But now he had lost a quarter of his brain which left a hole on his right side of the head

༄༅

The years rolled on and he started school. He was not a confident child and soon enough he was being bullied for, "being on the slow side". Well, after having a considerable head injury when so young, and four occasions now when he'd stopped breathing, I guess it would not be surprising that his mind would be a little slow in computing. But he was not a stupid child and he certainly didn't have any outward signs of mental disability. But the relentless bullying affected him, giving him mood swings and bouts of depression.

When he was about thirteen, his fourth death struck. Both Debbie and our youngest daughter Christine, now of primary school age, were at their weekly dance classes. I went with them because I was needed to take measurements for their costumes as we were close to an upcoming concert.

Both of my sons, Arthur and Kevin, were left at home to do their own thing. They were responsible kids and on this particular afternoon, (around five p.m.) they had decided to go to the local shops on their push bikes – about a ten-minute ride away. They had locked our family's four pet Sheltie dogs in the house (as we'd do when all going out together) and left. Clive was not due home until after seven that night.

Dance classes had finished around six p.m. and we headed home, not realising what had taken place only an hour earlier. I was shocked to find the house in darkness, with the dogs inside, unfed; I was angry with the boys for having been out so long, not even having left any notes to say where they'd gone. So I fed the dogs and prepared our own meals. It was coming up to six-fifty p.m. when I heard a knock on the front door. Thinking it was the boys, I was ready to get stuck into them, but it wasn't to be…

I opened the door to see a policeman standing there, his face was grim.

"Good evening," he said. "Do you have two boys by the names of Arthur and Kevin?"

"Yes, I do?" I replied, suddenly feeling sickly. "What have they done now?"

I was expecting him to say that they had been caught stealing, or something worse, and that they had been locked up. But it was much worse.

"I'm sorry to give you some bad news," he began, "but they've been in a very bad accident on Windsor Road. They've been taken to Parramatta Hospital. You should get there as soon as possible."

I was aghast; it must have showed on my face.

"I could take you there if you'd like," he kindly offered.

Knowing how close Clive was due to arriving, I declined.

"Thank you," I said, "but my husband should be home any minute. He'll be able to take me, thank you very much."

As soon as Clive got in I explained the situation and we drove immediately to the hospital. Luckily our younger son, Kevin, was not badly injured, only receiving lots of cuts and bruises: he was fortunate enough to come home with us that night. Poor Arthur, however, was in a very bad way. He was literally black and blue all over. Kevin was able to tell us what had happened…

"We decided to ride our bikes up to the local shopping centre to buy some music," he'd said. "We took the short cut to Windsor Road, where there's the slight bend, and we checked both ways for the traffic. We knew it was very busy at that time of night but we couldn't see beyond it, so we took a chance to cross it when there was a big gap between cars. As we started across, a car came slowly down the curb side towards us, when all of a sudden this Volvo sped up, overtaking the slow car! He hit me, throwing me over the slow car and back onto the pathway [the pedestrian walk], but Arthur was hit and thrown into the air, and sent about thirty meters down the road. Our bikes were a mangled wreck."

Luckily for the boys, there was a house right on the corner of that road in which an ambulance driver lived, and he was just about to leave for work when the two got hit. He rushed to them, giving Kevin the all-clear, then rushed to Arthur's side – who lay motionless.

Sadly, he was, in fact, dead.

The ambulance driver worked very hard to revive him until an ambulance arrived. Once Arthur was then tended to, this man went back to Kevin to talk to him about the situation. He'd told Kevin that Arthur had been dead for about three minutes; he couldn't find a pulse at first, but kept working on him until he took a breath. Then he took him to the waiting ambulance for them both to go to hospital.

I felt sick to the stomach. This was yet *another* take on his life. He'd survived, but only just.

When he was allowed home about a week later, all wrapped in bandages and still heavily bruised, Arthur told us what he'd experienced of his death.

"When my body was lying on the ground," he said, "I saw a man trying to revive me. I had a little giggle, thinking I wasn't coming back – I didn't want to 'cos I was happy where I was. I rose up high into the sky until I was above the clouds. Then a man in a white gown appeared; he looked like Jesus, saying, "You must go back, for it's not your time yet".

"But I don't want to go back," Arthur had said to him.

The heavenly man apparently had a smile on his lips and then said to him, "What about Heather?" This was a girl Arthur knew at school and had liked her a lot, so the question would've played on his heartstrings. "Don't you think she'll be upset if you stay here?"

Arthur then told us that with that, he'd felt himself being pulled backward into his body very quickly. This, I suppose, is when the ambulance man would have found Arthur's pulse.

It took months for his body to recover and some scars seemed to stay with him, but he was never really quite the same after that accident.

His final, and fifth death, was in September 1997, when he took his life under a train. This has already been mentioned in *My Encounters with the Spirit Word* and, of course, it is covered in a little more detail in the previous chapter.

So, these are the "near death" accounts of my eldest son's traumatic, turbulent life, shared with you at his request (from Spirit).

ಬಂಛ

Arthur, as the groom's Best Man

Australia Day at the Markets

Since writing my first book, one gift in particular finally returned – in full...

On Australia Day, I was attending a market at a local park in my home town on the Mid North Coast of NSW. Christine, came with me to sell her gift-ware range of dragons, gargoyles and Gothic fairies. We talked about doing readings, as well, for Christine was still reasonably new to her medium abilities and I was willing to get back into that part of my life I'd given away nearly thirty years ago. Also, by having both of us present, one of us could read for a client while the other managed the stall.

Our sales were just starting to pick up as a crowd arrived, when a lady of short stature, who we'll call Robin, came to enquire about our readings. Her daughter, of around twenty years, was with her and also interested in having a reading.

"Who does the card readings?" the lady asked.

"We both do," Christine replied. She then brought her around to our card table that was set out in the rear of our stall, where it could be more private for the clients. As is our custom, Christine suggested to Robin to have a look at each of the tarot decks to see which one she best resonated with. To give you an idea of why, I only had my plain deck while Christine had several deck designs. I always have my plain deck – or ordinary playing cards – as these are the very cards I was taught to read with by my Aunty May way back in the 1970's.

To me, these plain cards are like my 'bible deck' for they've never failed me. I also work with a couple of other decks nowadays, but I'm most comfortable with the plain ones. Unless a client already knows who they'd like to have read for them, the opportunity to choose which deck helps make the decision for them. Also, using a deck they like best will ultimately affect the positive flow of energies surrounding them.

Robin looked them over, not sure at first which set she wanted; then she saw my 'bible deck'.

"It's been a long time since I've had a reading with a plain deck of cards," she said. "I'll go with those."

I was thrilled and sat down opposite her to explain what to do and how I work with them, and she was fascinated.

Her daughter wanted to sit with her, which was fine, though they asked if we minded anyway.

We often get this question when two or more people want to be read for and, unless the client wishes to have a wholly private session, we are quite happy for them to have the company of friends or family.

"Oh no, that's quite alright," I assured her, and encouraged the daughter to grab the spare chair brought along for this exact reason. She sat just to her mother's left and slightly behind her. I began the reading as I always do; I mentally send a prayer to my spirit guides and angels, asking them to protect and guide me and help me to connect with the spiritual loved ones of the people I read for. As I started to tell Robin what I could see in the cards, a tall, dark-haired gentleman appeared beside the daughter. I sensed immediately that he was their relative.

The daughter noticed my eyes being drawn to the space on her left, and a little behind her.

"Can you see anyone with us?" she asked.

"Yes, a man," I replied, pleased that after so many years, a spirit was visible to me once again.

"What does he look like?" she asked.

I went on to describe him, saying that I felt he could be a grandfather or an uncle, but that I wasn't sure because he didn't speak to me at this stage.

Robin's eyes filled with tears, as though she knew, or sensed, who it was. She didn't clarify who she thought it might be, so I went on with the reading. He stayed beside them the whole time.

I was about to bring the reading to a close when she asked, "Is he still there?"

"Yes, and he is smiling. He must be pleased with your reading." Then I said something that must have meant a lot to her. "He has been watching over you for a couple of months now and is very proud of something that you have achieved recently."

Robin burst into tears. Her daughter tried reassuring her, then explained her mother's reaction.

"Of all the clairvoyant's that we have been to in the last twelve months, you are the only one who has ever picked up on her brother-in-law, whom she misses dreadfully. And now you have made us very happy. The tears are of joy, not sadness, and she has just been sitting for her nursing exams and was hoping that she will pass it."

In response to this, the man in spirit said, "She will pass, but only just."

I repeated his message, adding a little more to it from the other spiritual energies I was receiving. "I feel you will get around seventy-five to eighty per-cent in your results."

A few weeks later, early the following month, Robin rang me to give me an update of her exam test.

"Oh hi, guess what?" she cried excitedly. "My results are in! You were spot-on! I got seventy-eight per cent in my test!"

"That's great news!" I said.

"Thank you so much! I'll be in touch with you later in the year to see if anything has changed – and maybe you could read for my husband at the same time?" Robin cried.

I was very excited for her and agreed. I've since read for the family twice more, with great results.

The day in the park was great for both my daughter and I. We did a few readings between us and sold quite a lot of our goods. But the highlight for me was this earliest reading of the day, for this was the very first ghost, or spirit, as they like to be called, that I had seen since my book was published.

Until then, I had only seen glimpses here and there and sometimes, outlines of people, while some spirits were hard to make out. I couldn't stop smiling and thanking Spirit for their help and guidance. I know that I have to have confidence and patience, and that I will be given my gifts back slowly, as promised. With time, I will be strong again, of this I'm sure. Like all of us, I must work very hard to achieve this precious Gift of Seeing, and to respect the ways in which Divine energy work.

ಬಂಡ

By the beginning of the following month, while at a psychic fair, my daughter got her first official reading. She was very strong despite being in her early days of development and I was very pleased for her, as well as surprised at her strength. She had four readings this day and got better with each one, while I only had two readings. But again, I was spot-on in detail and also managed to see a couple of spirit people, although they didn't seem to want to say very much.

A couple of weeks later, I was called to the home of a beautiful lady, who spoke very highly of me, as she'd heard of my abilities to communicate with spirits.

She was a soft-spoken woman who'd lost her father some years ago. He came through with messages of love, which brought tears to her eyes. As with Robin, she'd gone to several other clairvoyants: none of them had mentioned him. She had been very close to him and missed him a lot, and had drawn much comfort from our 'three-way' conversation.

By now I felt I was getting much stronger, and also very proud to know that Lydia, who had helped to put me back on in this path, was watching over me, guiding me along. It was so exciting when *my Encounters with the Spirit World* was printed and ready for sale. I ordered quite a few, for I knew that a lot of my friends and family wanted one, too. Two of my local libraries ordered a copy, with one of them even organising a mini book launch for me!

ಸಂಞ

Lydia, my Beautiful Angel

I first met my angel in 2010 before *My Encounters with the Spirit World* was even written, let alone published. It was while I was washing up the dishes when two spirit ladies appeared to me on my left side, quietly standing by the bench. One was very robust with beautiful white hair, and the other one was slim, dainty in appearance though shorter, and whose hair looked like steel-coloured wool.

My kitchen joins with an informal eating and TV room and in the background there, I could hear my daughter, Christine, talking to someone.

"I want you to go and give Meg a message," the white-haired lady said.

"I can't. I don't know anyone called Meg," I replied, taken aback.

"Your daughter is talking to her on the phone. Please give her this message and she will understand."

I can't recall the actual message now, but I did as asked and went to Christine. Not wanting to interrupt her, I wrote the message on a piece of paper for her to read.

After a moment she paused in her conversation to see what I wanted, so I quietly said, "If you are talking to a lady called Meg, please give her this message."

She nodded, glancing at the note and continued chatting, so I returned to the kitchen sink, thinking I had done my duty for the spirit lady. Just as I was finishing up, I heard Christine say, "Okay then, we'll see you next Tuesday night."

I sensed she was about to hang up, but hadn't yet given the message to the person on the phone. So I hurried back over and pointed to the note, insisting she pass on this message. Then she said something that freaked me out.

"Oh, by the way, Meg, Mum would like to ask you something. Do you mind talking to her?"

Christine was waving me closer. Now I had not spoken with this lady before nor knew anything about her, so I was quite nervous about talking to her of the spirit lady.

"I'd rather it come directly from Mum, than through me," Christine finished and handed me the phone.

"Hello, Meg, is it?" I began, very unsure of myself.

"Yes," came the reply; she sounded like a nice lady and carefully I went on.

"Do you have two grandmothers in spirit?"

"Yes, I do!" she said. "Why do you ask?"

She didn't sound at all offended and seemed curious to know more.

"Well, it's just that I was standing at my kitchen sink, washing the dishes, when these two beautiful, lovely spirit ladies appeared at my side, saying that I need to get a message to you."

I went on to explain what had happened, describing them, too.

Meg could identify both correctly, though she didn't mention their names.

We talked for a little while and I learned that Meg was a medium. She was able to tell me why these two ladies had chosen me to pass on their message instead of going to her directly.

"You're being tested," she said. "If you can see them then you are ready to accept the Sight (of spirits) back into your life."

I was so happy! I went back to the sink after that call and drew an imaginary tick in the air, saying, "YES!" out loud with excitement. Not only did I see a couple of spirits *and* correctly pass on their message, but apparently I was now also ready to see more of them.

Then the same, white-haired lady came to me again.

"Now you will have to write a book," she said.

"A book?" I asked. "What would I write a book about?"

"You are to write a book about all of the readings you did in the past."

"But that's confidential, isn't it?"

"Don't worry about that," she added, "Just pick up your pen and paper; we'll tell you what to write. As long as you don't mention names or places without their permission, you will be safe. You were given this gift but you gave it back. We will guide you on what to write, and for each one that you write about, you will receive one of your gifts back."

This was exciting, but I still had no idea where to start, or how it should go. I didn't have to worry though, for like she said, she would be there to help me.

She described the colour of the book's cover – the specific three shades of white and purple fading from top to bottom. She said that it had to have nine spirits on the front. I was shown how it would look in a very clear vision, that has stayed with me to this day. She even told me how to sign the copies!

"You *must* write this book!" she insisted. "You have to get a message out to the world that if you are given (spiritual) gifts, it's for a reason. You are not to be afraid of them and you are *not* to give them up – not for anyone or for any reason!"

I listened to everything she said, a bit fearful that I could do this enormous task on my own. She must've sensed my concerns.

"Your daughter will help you," she said of Christine, (who was already a published author and was familiar with writing and publishing books). "It's got to get out there and with your daughter's help, it will."

༄༅

On the following Tuesday night at our friend's house, I met Meg as expected. She was sitting on the lounge with a couple of other people, yet I recognised her straight away, for she looked just like the white-haired spirit lady!

ଛଓ

Within days I sat down to write my stories. It was interesting to go back over those memories for they were from so long ago that it almost seemed a different lifetime! And then I had to get used to typing on the computer. Well, this was 'fun', but as the lady had said, my daughter Christine was on hand to help me.

So together we wrote and edited the inside pages, and then designed the artwork for the cover. We found nine pictures of real people, who are mostly of my family, and who are now in spirit. With a lot of effort, we managed to get the right shades of white to purple, as well as the look and colour of the text in the title.

It was funny because, whenever Christine changed the words of something I'd written, (she knows how to structure sentences together so the scene reads properly) she, or I, or both, would get very clear, "Ah, no, that's not right," vibes from Spirit – it had to be said according to how Spirit wanted it said.

Then, many months later and a few days after we had finally finished the book, the same white-haired lady appeared again, telling me I had to go to a publisher called Hay House. As I didn't read any books, only magazines, I wasn't familiar with publishing companies and sort of forgot about them. However, unbeknown to me, Christine had also picked up the 'vibe' *Hay House*.

She reminded me to enquire with them when she was telling me about the publishing process, so we looked up Hay House on the internet and soon sent the manuscript off. Unfortunately, due to tight scheduling, they could not take it on at the time, however they sent me to Balboa

Beautiful Spirits

Press, a division of the parent company, who welcomed my book with excitement.

So I say that *My Encounters with the Spirit World* is Spirit's book – made with our help. But this book, *Beautiful Spirits*, is mine, helped along with spirit when I needed it.

☯

One bright, sunny morning, after my book had been published, I was having breakfast with my husband when the same, beautiful, spirit lady appeared on my right again. Even though she had stayed with me through the months of writing, I still did not know her name and though I'd asked her many times, she'd always said that it wasn't important and that I wasn't to worry about it.

It seemed an impossible question to ask her yet again, so this time I said, "Okay, I have done what you have asked me to do and my book is now with the publishers. I can do no more for you, so can you now tell me your name because I can't keep telling people, "the white-haired spirit lady told me to write this book…". And I would like to thank you by your name."

She hesitated, seeming to think about telling me. Then she gave a big sigh.

"Okay, it's Lydia," she grunted (yes, grunted).

"Thank you," I replied, feeling much happier. But I wasn't sure I'd heard her properly, for 'Lydia' was not a familiar name to me. "Did you say Lydia, or Libya?"

With her arms crossed, she half smiled and said, "Lydia."

"Thank you," I said, before she faded away. I was still wondering later that day if I had clearly heard her answer. Did she really say "Libya"? Or maybe this was where she was born, or perhaps lived? Feeling confused, and uncertain if she was having a joke with me, I rang Meg, hoping she could confirm what I had heard.

When I told her what had happened that morning, she laughed out loud.

"What does it mean?" I asked. "What's so funny?"

"Oh yes! Lydia was indeed her name!" Meg said, with a chuckle in her voice. "No one outside her family ever called her this name as people only knew her by "Elizabeth"!"

"Oh, so I could've called her Libby or Betty?" I asked.

"Oh no!" Meg firmly replied. "She hated being called those names. Everyone who knew her only called her Elizabeth."

In hearing this news, I felt quite honoured to know that my spirit-lady had given me the family's 'pet' name for her, a rather personal touch that filled me with joy.

৪০তঃ

Back then, neither Lydia or the other lady had ever appeared to me as angels. Within a couple or so years of the first book being published, Meg, sadly, died.

Then, around July 2018, leading up to this second book being published, all three came to me together – Lydia had come to say "goodbye", it seemed.

She stood closest to me, with the other two standing a little beside and behind her. All were smiling at me.

"Thank you for all of what you've done with the books," Lydia said. "We are grateful that you've put the message out there for people to know and learn not to give up the Gifts they are given by Spirit."

I felt them each give me a loving hug, which made me feel wonderfully warm all over.

They turned sideways, and that's when I saw their magnificent wings… beautiful angel's wings. Then the three gently glided up, presumably to Heaven.

I'm not expecting to see her anymore, as her work with me is now done.

But you never quite know…

৪০তঃ

My Cousin in New Zealand

In May 2012, Clive and I went to New Zealand, primarily to visit my cousin, Gerry, who was very sick with cancer and also suffering Parkinson's disease. Clive and I love model trains and live steam and while visiting this wonderful country, we were fortunate to see a model railway exhibition just down the road from Gerry's house. We also enjoyed a scenic ride on the Tieri Gorge, a four-hour round-trip steam train journey from Dunedin to Pugerangi, through magnificent mountainous country, over trestle bridges and several tunnels. The second steam ride is called the Seasider, which follows the coastline in the opposite direction and is also a four-hour round-trip journey. I urge anyone travelling to this part of New Zealand that they must go on these trips to experience the beautiful countryside.

Gerry introduced us to his neighbour, Sue, (who lived next door to him and who looked after his general needs), and also to his good friends, Peter, and wife, Alison, who were wonderful company for him. We soon discovered that Peter had a great singing voice and both he and Gerry loved to sing together. Our evenings were especially memorable when we all sat in Gerry's lounge room, around the open fireplace, listening to the two harmonise wonderfully together.

One morning I was having a cup of tea on an armchair in front of this open fireplace. Gerry was having his breakfast on the lounge opposite me, with his back to the window: we were talking about my first book. There was just the two of us, at first…

"Do you believe this type of thing?" he had asked, genuinely interested.

"Yes," I said: naturally I did.

"Can you really see people?"

"Yes," I repeated. Of course I could, for three people had now appeared behind him – quite transparent and only from the waist up, but they looked familiar to me. One of them was his sister, Lena, who had lived in England until she'd died from a severe illness in old age some years earlier.

Then the usual question came next.

"Can you see anybody with me now?"

"Yes, you've got three people with you now. Your sister is standing behind your right shoulder."

"Really?" he cried in amazement.

"And your Mum is standing right there behind you now," I added. Then I pointed to his left shoulder. "And your Dad is standing right there."

"Really? You can really see them?" he eagerly exclaimed.

"Yes!"

"What are they saying?"

"Well, nothing, they're just smiling. His mother wrapped her arms lovingly around him.

"And your Mum's giving you a big hug. Can you feel the warmth around your shoulders, or any pressure like you're getting a hug?"

He paused to feel for the sensation, and then…

"Ah, yes I think I can!"

His Dad was smiling. I don't know what he was smiling about, although I think he was indicating that he was very proud of him and of what he had achieved. But I have also wondered (much later) if it was because he knew Gerry was going over into Spirit soon.

His parents – my aunt and uncle respectively – and his sister, had lived in England all their lives and to my knowledge, had never come to New Zealand. Yet in Spirit, they knew where he was and they'd had no difficulty with our physical distance in finding him; they could be with him no matter where he was.

Earthly locations don't have the same impact of distance and travel in the spirit realm. Nor do they cause anyone any problems in finding you. If your loved one lived in one part of the world or country to you and had never been to your home before they'd died, or if you'd moved after their death, they can, and will, still find you. It's *you* they want, *you* they love. They get to see your home simply by you being in it, even if it's a new house you moved to after they've died.

Naturally, Gerry was overjoyed with the news of his Dad, Mum and sister, for he loved them still and had missed his family terribly.

෴

Two weeks after our arrival back home in Australia I started to worry about his health. I felt the presence of his Mum and Dad, who were trying to tell me to contact him. So I tried calling him but only got his answering machine. After several attempts to ring him over the following days, with no replies and no one else being able to tell me his situation, I started worrying even more, to the point of crying with frustration. I just *knew* something was wrong!

I ended up ringing his doctor's office, to learn that he had collapsed in the street and gone into hospital. Eventually I was able to talk with him by telephone to his hospital room, though his speech sounded dreadful and slurred. I believe he cheered up when hearing from me and we talked a couple of more times before he recovered enough to go home.

Soon after this incident, I was told that Gerry had been admitted to a nursing home. I felt more at ease then because I knew he would be well looked after.

Four months later, he passed away at seventy-five years old. He is no longer in pain or discomfort but is now free of disease, and is now with his family in spirit.

ಸಿಲ

Cousin Gerry

The Mischievous Child

Around August, Christine and I went to stay with my niece, Michelle, in the far outer suburbs of Sydney,
for the weekend. She'd arranged for me to do readings for some friends of hers on the Friday night, (while she and Christine would be busy with a play being performed in Penrith). I was to also do more readings the next morning.

Michelle said that the first of the readings (on the Friday night) was at the house of her childhood friend, Sissy, which, she'd added, was haunted. This experience was an eye-opener for me and it took me by surprise. It was about five o'clock in the evening when my sister and I arrived, slightly earlier than expected, but Sissy said it was okay and showed us to the lounge, where we waited while they prepared the kids' meals. Almost straight away I could see glimpses of spirits walking around, with one man walking out the front door as though nobody else was around! After about fifteen minutes though, I felt someone else's presence.

"Sam," they said. I didn't know if the spirit person was a male or female, nor their age or anything else about them. I just knew that they wanted to be known to the girls in the house.

The feeling was strong enough that I went to the kitchen where Sissy and her friend, Emma, were cooking.

"Does anyone know a Sam?" I asked.

A shocked look came over their faces, and they looked at each other with their mouths wide open.

"Yes," they both replied.

"Okay, well I've just heard someone say that name to me." I said. "I didn't know if it was a male or a female that I heard. It was just the name."

"Really?!" they cried.

"Yes. In fact, I've seen quite a few spirits wandering around already."

"Yes, other people have seen them too," said Emma. "They are friendly spirits and won't harm us."

"They've been here as long as we have lived in this house," Sissy added. "We don't know who they are but they don't frighten us. We think they are protecting us."

"They're probably your loved ones watching over you. I just saw what looked like an elderly man walk out the front French doors, too."

"We've seen him too!" said Sissy, agreeing. "We think he was the original owner of the place."

I went back to the lounge to give the girls a chance to finish making the meal, but even as I entered the room I heard the name, "Sam," said again. Sitting on the lounge, I sensed who it was more strongly.

"Tell them Sam's here!" she said.

So I returned to the girls in the kitchen.

"I'm sorry to bother you again," I began. "Sissy, who is Sam please?"

She looked at Emma quite oddly.

"It's just that I've had a little girl come up to me and tell me to tell you that she's here."

"Emma's friend was called Sam," she replied, "but she died years ago."

"Well, maybe they're trying to tell me your friend is here," I said.

They were smiling but were stunned with the news.

Sam, however, wasn't done yet...

My first official reading of the evening was with a lady named Kelly. We were shown to a bedroom (the only place spare for privacy) and began, though neither of us were ready for what was to come. After showing her what to do with the cards I felt spirit people gathering around me. This house seemed to attract them and it was fun to be doing this here. I wouldn't mind doing more readings like this, for the atmosphere of the spirits were kind and friendly.

As I started her reading, I picked up on a male spirit. He was a young man, who seemed to be a close friend of Kelly's when he was alive.

"I feel there's a young man in spirit with you. He's standing over there," I said, pointing to a corner on her right. "I feel he was close to you and that he was in a car accident. He's showing me a motorbike, and I sense there was a motorbike involved in this accident."

"Yes, I know who you're talking about."

He showed me a few scenes (like those of a film clip) of what happened in the accident; I saw him sitting in the back seat of a car, behind the driver, when a motorbike ran into him.

"He was sitting in the back seat," said Kelly, unaware what I was seeing. "The motorbike ran into his part of the car where he was sitting."

"Well, he's said to tell you that everything's fine, and that he's happy where he is."

Kelly nodded, happy with the news.

The next particular card I turned over was the ten of Diamonds, this told me of a drowning incident. At the same time, I heard a young girl say, "This is how I died."

"Do you know of a young girl that drowned?" I asked Kelly.

She looked startled and put her hands to her mouth.

"Yes! Wow!" she said. "That was Sam, Emma's friend, who drowned when she was about eight or nine years old!"

I sat back in my chair, feeling quite excited. After having heard her name called earlier, now I was given some background in to her passing.

"I feel like she is saying that she was pushed by accident before slipping into the water. Do you know if this is what happened?"

"I wouldn't know," she said, clearly thinking on it. "Emma told me about it years ago; I don't remember that far back. It happened when they were young."

"Well don't worry about her," I said, not wanting to press her. "She is saying that she is very happy where she is and she is healthy."

We let the topic of Sam slide as I continued with the rest of Kelly's reading. When done, she thanked me, quite happy with the outcome.

The next reading was for Emma.

As she sat down, I promptly picked up the card that indicated a drowning and, showing it to her, I said, with a grin, "I won't tell you about Sam's drowning."

Emma looked shocked. "Why?" she asked.

"Can you see this card?" I asked her.

"Yes. What does it mean?"

"Well, if you see it from this way," I explained, showing her the Ten of Diamonds, "it indicates a drowning. It was what came up in Kelly's reading." I briefed her about that part of the reading, for otherwise I don't repeat the details of private sessions with others. "I asked Kelly if she knew who it was," I said. "She told me it was possibly your friend Sam."

Emma was amazed.

"She must have been meant to get that message because if I turn it this way up, it has a different meaning."

"Oh wow," she said, smiling. I returned the card to the deck and gave them to Emma to shuffle. As it turned out, the Ten of Diamonds reappeared in her reading, this time in reverse.

"Ah, see?" I said, pointing to it. "This means you are going overseas or on a holiday – you're travelling to, or over, some water."

"Yes, I am planning on going on holidays," she said.

"Now, you could not have had the drowning side of the card come up *and* the water-travel side in the same reading, because they're on the same card. *You're* going on a holiday, which means Sam had to come through Kelly's reading, as you would not have been told of her due to this message here for you. In other words, for Sam to have gotten through to you, she had to come through Kelly's reading, and this way Spirit could still tell you of your upcoming travel."

Emma was flabbergasted. Smiling, she said, "Oh, well I'm glad Sam is still around! I'm really happy that she's alright!"

Sissy came in next, which surprised me, for I thought her daughter was the one I was to read for following Emma.

"She's just lost one of her friends," Sissy explained of her daughter, "and doesn't feel that she can handle it if you brought her through. So I'm taking her place, if that's okay."

"Yes, sure," I replied. "Sit down and I'll see what I can do for you."

In the course of her reading, some members of her family came through, which pleased her to have had this contact with them. Towards the end of the session I asked her if she had any questions that I hadn't answered yet.

"Please ask me now and I'll try and help you."

It only took her a few minutes to respond.

"I was wondering if you could tell me if my daughter's friend that passed over is happy, 'cos we all miss her." It was clear this friend was special, for her sadness overwhelmed her and tears began to fill her eyes.

I mentally 'looked' for her, sensing a lovely young girl in her teens, who conveyed her answers to me.

"Oh yes," I said. "She is very happy."

"Can you see her?" Sissy asked, brightening.

"Yes, she is standing over there. She is teaching some small children with what looks like to be building blocks, with letters on them."

Sissy gave a little gasp, putting her hands to her mouth.

"They are sitting around a child's small table and chair set and she is leaning over them, pointing to each block, saying, "C.A.T. – this spells 'cat'. She loves this job."

Her tears overflowed. "Before she died," she gently began, "she used to say, "Next year I'm planning to go to TAFE to learn child care". She wanted to look after and care for children."

I smiled as I turned towards the corner, watching the friend. "Well, she's very happy now because she has got her wish to do just what she wanted and doesn't need to go to TAFE. She's also telling me to tell your daughter not to worry herself over her death, and to get on with her life. She has to be strong or her health will go down. "Tell her I'm fine and very happy", she says," I relayed to Sissy. "She tells me it was her time to go over."

Sissy was relieved and very happy. As she was my last reading for the night, we left the room together, still chatting.

"If you want me to come back at any stage, I will read for your daughter. I feel she needs to have one," I said.

"Oh you definitely will be back, and thank you so much for coming all of this way for us!"

"That's alright! I've really enjoyed it. This is a wonderful place to pick up on Spirit."

On leaving the room, who should come down the hall but her depressed daughter!

"Guess what? Your friend is very happy and is teaching small children, but I'll tell you all about it later," Sissy said quite spritely.

I wanted to encourage the daughter, knowing she'd take it on board more readily if she heard it from me. "Yes, and you are to get on with your life. Stop worrying and be happy."

She sort of started to smile – shyly.

"The next time I come down this way I'll do your reading. Do you mind if I ask you a favour?"

"No, what is it?" she replied.

"Your friend has just told me to give you a hug from her. Do you mind if I give you a hug on her behalf?"

"Okay," she said, shrugging her shoulders.

I wrapped my arms around her, giving her the warm hug that her dear friend wanted to have done in my place, but which was a bit difficult due to her spiritual form.

"Mind," I added gently, "this is from her, not me."

Thankfully, she seemed to accept the hug as being from her friend in spirit.

Back in the kitchen, I offered to sign my book for Sissy.

"Oh yes please!" she cried excitedly, taking her copy from out of a drawer. She put it down on the bench top.

"Do you mind if I show you around the back area of the house first?" she asked. "Mum asked me to show it to you."

I learned then that this was actually her mother's house, not Sissy's, and that she was only looking after it while her mother was visiting Sissy's younger sister in Queensland.

"Okay. If you wish," I answered, remembering that this place was said to be haunted.

It felt strange walking around the home, as I only went to read cards for them, not go on a sort of private ghost tour. I was certainly not frightened, nor did I feel threatened. If anything, I felt honoured for the opportunity to meet their 'house spirits'.

The first room they took me to was the youngest child's bedroom.

"Can you see anyone?" Sissy asked me as I walked in.

I looked back towards the door we had just entered, seeing a lady standing there; she wasn't fully in view, but enough that I could make her out.

"Well, there's a tall lady just in the doorway," I said, "and I don't think she's very happy…"

"Mmm, I thought so," she said. "We've seen her before too! I just wanted some sort of confirmation, I think."

The spirit lady was now very angry. "GET OUT OF MY ROOM!" she shouted at me, knowing I could see her.

"Okay, sorry," I said to her, rather cheekily.

"What?" asked Sissy, puzzled.

Already I was making for the door.

"She's telling me to get out of her room!" I repeated for Sissy's benefit.

"Oh?" came her surprised response.

"She's okay," I added. "She means no harm to anyone. It's me, 'cos I'm a stranger to her."

We chuckled together and walked to the bathroom next. The full figure of a transparent old man awaited us.

Can you see anyone in here?" she asked again. By now, Sissy's friends Emma and Kelly had joined us, and they were watching me eagerly.

"Yes. There is a man standing here," I said, pointing at the door. "He is okay and doesn't mind me here. He is friendly. I think he is keeping an eye on everyone."

"That's it!" Emma said determinedly, clutching her dressing gown tightly around her waist. "I'm not going in for my shower now!"

The sentiments were the same for them all.

"It's okay," I said, smiling. "He won't hurt you and he won't look at you." Of course, I had to hope this was true, for my memory of my brother-in-law watching me as I changed into my pyjamas so many years ago was another thing altogether (described in my first book).

The next room she took me to was decorated in pink and was the bedroom for Sissy's middle child, whom I hadn't seen yet. As I went in, I saw the semi-transparent figure of a young spirit girl, which seemed to be playing with her daughter's toy's.

"Oh, there's a little girl in here. She's playing with the toys," I said, before they could ask me the same question yet again.

"Can you tell how old she is?" one of the women asked.

"Possibly around eight or nine, or even ten years old," I said. "Has your daughter ever seen her?"

"Yes," Emma answered on Sissy's behalf. "When she was younger she used to talk to her. We could hear her chatting away."

"Does she still talk to her?" I enquired.

"I'm not sure," said Emma. "I'll go and get her for you."

Now, I was expecting Sissy's daughter to be around the age of four or five, maybe even six, but certainly not older. This was going to be my first time seeing this daughter, (named 'Katie', here) and when she arrived at the room, I could see that she was about the same age as the spirit child. It felt a little weird to me.

"Hello, what is your name?" I said to her.

She was a beautiful girl and a bit shy with me. She sort of hid behind Emma, not really answering me.

"Do you ever play with a little girl in this room?" I gently asked her.

"I used to a long time ago," Katie said very quietly.

"Well, she is still here and playing with your toys now. Does she tell you to make a mess like this?"

She shook her head slowly, whispering, "No."

"Do you play with her quietly and do you make the mess?"

"Yes," she murmured, nodding.

"Do you know what her name is?" Sissy asked me.

"I'll ask her," I said and turned to the spirit girl. "What's your name, Sweetie?"

"Annie," or "Sammy," she said in a small voice; I wasn't sure which.

"It sounds like Annie, or Sammy; it's not clear for me to pick," I explained and then, to settle her nerves, I said to Katie, "It's okay to play with her. She won't harm you."

Just then, I felt a tickling sensation on both of my thighs, just above the kneecaps. It was something I didn't expect happening and I jumped out of my wits. I vigorously started rubbing the awful sensation away.

"Leave me alone!" I shouted to the spirit girl, who had decided I would be fun to tease. "I don't like being tickled, especially there!"

The women looked startled.

"It's okay," I said. "The spirit girl was tickling my legs, and I hate being tickled. She's stopped now. I think it's time to get out of this room."

On leaving, I felt this almighty scratch gouge down my back – she'd dragged her fingernails down with such force that it had hurt. I yelled with pain, and shock.

"Okay! I'm leaving!" I insisted, racing for the door.

We returned to the kitchen, which was just opposite the pink bedroom, where I told the women what the spirit girl had done.

They laughed, thinking it was funny, but it didn't feel funny to me at all. I didn't realise that the spirit girl had followed me, too. I thought she had stayed in the bedroom, playing. But oh no, not her. Little did I know what she would do next, and this is where she really tried to scare me.

On the whole, I realised she was only being mischievous, just like many kids can be, but while I stood next to the bench top, ready to sign Sissy's book, she interfered again. Unaware of her presence, I took my special pen from my purse.

I love this pen. It's metallic silver in colour and has a miniature gold angel on the end. I showed it to them, explaining how my late son, Arthur, had asked me to buy it (from in Spirit). As I opened the front cover, I started to feel strange. I don't know how to describe my feelings; I just knew there was more to come, almost like a premonition of something about to go wrong...

Very slowly I started to write "*...To Dear Sill...*" it was meant to be "*Dear Siss-*". I forced my hand to stop. I could see, and feel, this was not me writing; it was someone else. I was very shaky; my whole body was quivering as though I had tiny electrical shocks passing through me, and the writing itself was like that of a child or a very elderly person.

"I'm sorry," I said to Sissy, "but this is mad. This is not my writing. Someone else is writing this for me. I've never had this happen before." I showed her the problem. "See what I'm doing? It's spelling out 'Silly', not 'Sissy', and I will try and find out who it is before I go on."

I shook my arms a few times, stretching them out so tightly until it hurt, all the while saying, "Go away. Leave me alone." After a short while I felt a little calmer, and then turned to the mischievous spirit.

"Who are you and what is your name?" I demanded.

"It's me, Anne," said the little girl.

I wasn't sure if she said her name was Anne, or Annie, but it could also have been Sammy. Or maybe she had a second name, like Samantha Anne. All I know is that it was an "Ann" name which came through. It may, possibly, have been the little girl, Sam, who'd drowned, but this wasn't made clear to me. In fact, I was beginning to feel that the spirits wanted me to go. All I wanted to do now was sign the book and leave.

"Well I'm not going to sign this until you leave me alone!"

It took me several minutes to sort out the strange energy that had been put on me and when it settled, I said, "Right, I'll give it another try."

I took control of my senses, along with a deep breath and, picking up my trusty little pen, said a prayer under my breath to my guides to help me write properly. Looking at the spoiled start, angry that she had interfered, I deliberately wrote the rest of Sissy's name over the top of the original one, and added behind it…

"*from Anne…*"

I didn't want anyone reading this later to think I was being a smarty-pants when signing the book, which was quite possibly what the girl had wanted.

Then, willing all to go right, I took a new line and wrote…

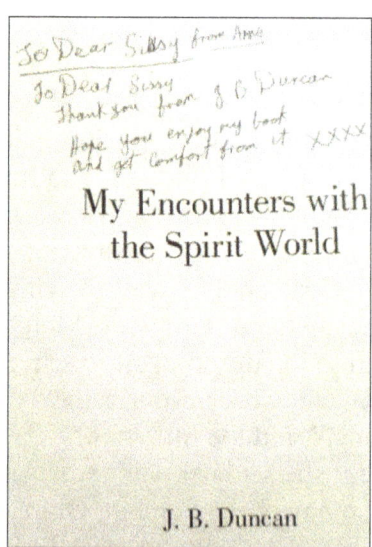

Sissy's signed book

Perfect.

Beautiful Spirits

I acknowledged Spirit, sending a big thanks to my guides, angels and loved ones for their help. Sissy, Emma and Kelly each looked at the two signings, amazed with the result.

"Wow!" Kelly said. "Look at the difference! They are definitely different!"

I apologised again and said that I would give her a replacement book next time I came down to Sydney, but they refused, saying, "We're happy with the way it was meant to be and we think it's hilarious."

They understood my dilemma and couldn't stop thanking me for making the journey all the way down, as it was a long four hours away from home. They said that they would try and get more people for me next time, to make my trip worthwhile. I was so pleased, and I'll be looking forward to visiting these ladies in this house again, for not only were they very happy with the outcome, I was very happy to know my gifts really are getting stronger, particularly with each reading.

I often thank my spirit guides for showing me the right 'door' to walk through, for I know that they are with me all the time. I feel great!

༺༻

Early Saturday morning I was up and ready. I knew it was going to be a busy day for me and straight after breakfast, my first reading for the day had arrived. I brought members of the client's family through, which pleased her immensely. A small child came through, too, whom she acknowledged to be that of her older brother, who'd died at the age of eighteen months.

As these experiences can be very personal, you have to respect a client's feelings. I can't reveal the details of my conversations that morning as I didn't ask them about sharing their stories here, but everyone did seem happy with their readings.

༺༻

Tina's Visit

In September 2012, a week before going on a booked ghost tour at Quarantine Station (see next chapter, "*The Lost Girl*") we had received terrible news about my niece, Tina. I had just finished my dinner when Michelle, my other niece, who was close to Tina, telephoned me.

"Aunty Joyce?" she began. "Tina's in hospital. She's taken an overdose and has been rushed there a few hours ago. She's on life-support at the moment, though it doesn't look good."

This was easily a minimum five-hour drive into the city for us from where we live and, as there was nothing we could do but wait, we stayed home until further notice.

The very next day while I was sitting at the breakfast table, having a cup of coffee, I heard Tina's voice talking to me.

"Don't worry Aunty Joyce," she said, sounding calm, "I've gone over now and I'm very happy."

At first I wondered what she meant, for I was miles away in my own thoughts. Then I realised that Tina was standing on my right side, approximately one metre away, her appearance clearly visible, and telling me that she had left her body in the hospital. I immediately looked up at the oven clock to see what time it was. It was 11:30 am.

"Okay, thank you, Sweetheart," I replied.

Gently she faded away.

However, over the next couple of hours I felt Tina was trying to give me some kind of specific message, for I could see her right hand being held by someone. She appeared to be squeezing that person's hand pretty hard, too.

Around four o'clock that afternoon, Michelle rang me back.

"Hi Aunty Joyce," she said, sounding tired and a little sad. "Tina's not any better. She's showing no signs of improvement" She briefed me of the updates. "I've spent most of the morning with Tina, but I feel that she's gone."

Around nine o'clock the following morning, I received the phone call from Michelle that I was sort of expecting.

"Hello Aunty Joyce?"

"Yes Pet, what is it? Has she gone? Has her body finally given out?"

"Yes, Aunty Joyce," she said, her voice breaking. "The hospital staff turned off the life-support machine at two-fifty this morning. They checked it with me first. I was holding her hand and it went limp, and I knew there was nothing left there. So I gave them the okay." She broke into tears. "I had to Aunty Joyce! It's what she wanted!"

"I know," I said soothingly. "What time was it when she went limp?"

"Two-thirty."

"And were you holding her right hand?" I asked, curious to understand the vision I'd seen.

"No," she replied, "I was holding her left hand. Why do you want to know?"

I told her of Tina's visit to me that morning, particularly of her squeezing someone's hand very hard, but that I couldn't be sure what it meant.

Michelle sort of chuckled and said, "Oh, that was Kathryn's hand!"

Kathryn is Tina's older sister, who had shared those final, early hours with Michelle beside Tina in the hospital. It's worth mentioning here that Michelle believes in Spirit and in things that cannot always be explained by science, so she didn't find this experience unusual.

"She almost squeezed the life out of it, which frightened her!" Michelle added, of Tina. "Kathryn didn't know what to do. She just freaked out!"

"So that explains what I saw," I said, glad now that the vision made sense.

"Yeah!" Michelle laughed. "I told her to just stay calm, and that it was probably Tina's way of saying goodbye to her."

I was about to say the same thing! It was so sweet.

"Well she's gone to a better place," I said. "She'll be much happier now."

"I know," she said, softly crying. "She didn't want to live anymore."

We spoke for a while longer. As Tina's Executor, Michelle was now to arrange a funeral service for her, even though Tina hadn't wanted one. It was hectic for her, though she handled it all very well. This, of course, was a week out from us all going to the Quarantine Station in Manly. As Tina's funeral was being held on the Monday morning and the group ghost tour was on the Saturday evening immediately beforehand, my own two daughters and I were there at Michelle's place for three days.

On the Sunday night, Michelle asked if any of us wished to say something at the service, as both she and Kathryn planned on speaking at it too. I said that I wanted to speak, but that I didn't know yet what I'd say. I planned on thinking of the right words after breakfast, before going to the service.

Around five a.m. on Monday morning, I was woken by the sound of my name…

"Hello? Aunty Joyce?"

Tina stood by the bed, smiling.

At first, I tried to ignore her as the sun wasn't quite up yet and I wanted the sleep.

"Aunty Joyce, I want you to say some things for me at the service today," she said.

I stalled, really wanting to stay under the warm blankets.

"Aunty Joyce," she persisted.

This went on for a while.

"What?" I finally replied in my head.

"I have some words I need you to say to my family."

I could tell that my mind was awake by now and I couldn't rest any more, so I got up.

It had just turned six a.m. and the sun was starting to peep through the window. I went quietly through to the kitchen table, armed with my pen and paper, hoping not to wake anyone. I sat down and started to write what *I* wanted to say at the service, when Tina kept telling me what she wanted me to say on her behalf.

"I can't say that!" I said on several occasions.

"But why not? It's true!" she'd countered, or, "they deserve to hear it anyway!"

There was a lot I couldn't say, as she was very angry (with her family, particularly her Mum) and she was upset with me because I wouldn't repeat it. I did, however, manage to calm her down with promising to say as much as I could without upsetting anybody.

When the time came for the eulogies, my nieces Michelle and Kathryn were too upset to say their speeches. I was determined to not let Tina down and when it came my turn, I had to repeat to myself, "I'm not going to cry. I'm not going to cry."

But of course – what happened after I started talking? I broke down and cried! I did, however, get through my speech with Tina's help, as she was standing by my side, saying, "Go on Aunty Joyce, keep going. You are doing fine."

By the end of my speech, I felt calm come over me and I said a quiet "thank you" to her for helping me through it all, which I think made her proud.

As the service was closing, a funny thing happened. Tina was a big fan of the Western Sydney football team, the Bulldogs, and she had a huge team flag that she adored. Michelle had draped it over the stand that held the coffin and while the song, *"Who Let the Dogs Out"* played, the flag suddenly dropped off one side. Everyone saw it fall, but what they didn't see was why… Tina had stormed up to her coffin.

"That's mine and I'm taking it with me!" she said, pulling the left corner of the flag. It was so comical to see her determination in taking it back.

Since then, Tina has been to visit me occasionally and she's been with Michelle lots of times, looking after her almost daily. She's very proud of Michelle for the lovely funeral she gave her and for having stuck by her when she had needed someone to talk to.

༄༅

Tina

The Lost Girl

Two days before Tina's funeral I went to the haunted Quarantine Station at Manly, located on the North Head of Sydney harbour. Both of my two daughters and my niece, Michelle, went too, along with several friends. We made a total of eighteen and most of us were spiritually tuned-in in one way or another, which made for a very interesting evening…

  This was my first 'real' Ghost Tour and the grounds and buildings of this historic site are reputed to be one the most haunted in Australia. Q Station (as it is often called), operated as a quarantine station from 14th August 1832 to 29th February 1984. People arriving in Sydney (by boat), who were thought to have an infectious disease, would be sent here for up to forty days, or until they were considered safe enough for release into the community. Years later, some buildings on the land were also used as a hotel and even today, the public can make use of convention facilities as well as accommodation there.

  On this occasion, I was looking forward to the evening and also to writing about it, but the spirits have blocked me from saying much at all, for every time I have thought of what to say, my mind gets a blankness of the memory. It seems I have been limited to what I could see, hear or feel that night, for even when recalling it in a conversation, it's like I only see a room in darkness. There were buildings I could go into and not see spirits with my eyes, yet I could sense them, while in other areas I *could* hear them, or see them, but not much else. My Spirit Guides only allowed me to see or hear some encounters, perhaps in order to protect me, for there is a lot of dark and negative energy on these grounds, where, during its years of public service, many people have died horrible deaths.

A spirit did tell me that other people have already written books on the "ghosts" of Q Station and that they didn't need mine to add to the list. Basically, I am to leave them in peace. All I am allowed to say, however, is that it was well worth the experience of being there – the highlight for me being when I was able to help a very frightened young spirit girl cross over.

Our tour group was taken into a wing of an old hospital – one of several buildings on this large estate. With help from Christine, who can share some detail to my 'blankness', this little girl had followed us up from the Inhalation Chamber, (a smallish type of den where new arrivals were chemically treated before being given entry to the rest of the station). Christine was in her own small 'group' of spirit children, each of them apparently holding her hands on the walk up the hill to this hospital.

My daughter had therefore lagged behind us all (in her words, "for the sake of the kids keeping up with her") and she'd missed out on hearing the introduction of either of these wings. She would soon tell me of her experience in approaching the hospital, but for the time being, our guide, Lauren, told us she would only take us into this left wing, for the other one (directly opposite) was known to have a very aggressive, almost evil, male presence in it.

Lauren then requested that we leave our hand-held lanterns outside by the near wall, where she would resume her talk. It should be noted here that apparently many of the spirits of Q Station don't like bright light – or lights at all – so much of the time that we were indoors, we were able to see our surroundings by the soft light shining from the EXIT signs. So we set down our lamps and went into the darkened room.

Once inside, Lauren asked us to each stand by one of the beds there and then went on to explain a brief history of the rooms here and, of course, of the spirits commonly known to haunt them. As for Christine, she and her little 'brood' were now approaching the twin buildings and, as she later explained, the children began to grow distinctly frightened, particularly of the wing on their right. Bear in mind that Christine had not yet heard of the mean, aggressive presence next door. She'd had to spend some time assuring the kids that they'd be safe if they stayed within the ring of lamp light and that the angels would protect them, too.

She eventually entered our wing quietly, closing the door behind her until it 'clicked' in place. Then she went midway down the room to find an empty bed to stand by and listen with the rest of us to Lauren's talk. Our guide revealed that even when the station was open as a working hospital, people experienced ghostly activity. Now, none of us were near the entrance during this session and yet, even while Lauren spoke, this very door opened wide enough to accommodate a small person. It then closed again, as though whoever had just entered the room had thought to shut it behind them!

"Ah," Christine murmured softly, and her eyes followed an invisible presence down the floor to her side. She nodded and appeared to offer her hand for holding.

Lauren paused as though to give Christine a chance to say something.

"It's one of the kids," she said. "They're scared out there." She briefed us of what had happened of her walk up from the wash-shed; "A group of them came with me – they wanted to help show me around the place. But they don't like it up here. They told me that there's a, "big scary man over there", who, I feel, is very nasty. He likes to scare people who visit here, but in life, he also didn't like children much, or was impatient with them. He was very strict with kids and wouldn't hesitate to cane them." She also added that, "In their spiritual realm here, he's *very* nasty, *very* scary – he delights in the terror."

She looked at the invisible child beside her.

"This little one couldn't wait any longer," she added. "She's terrified of the scary man next door. She wants to be in here where she feels safer with us."

Presumably the child settled with Christine and Lauren continued with her talk, inviting us to then wander around the interior for a while before we were to move on to the next destination.

It was during this 'free time' that I was drawn to Christine and this little girl who, now I had the opportunity to concentrate on her, I could sense myself. Both of us could describe the colour and design of her late Victorian dress, with its pink, vertical stripes and lace finish on the collar and its short sleeves. She even wore a type of pinafore over the top, and a pretty yet simple long white ribbon in her hair.

Also drawn to us was one of the other mediums, a lovely lady who had tuned into this beautiful child. Between the three of us, we learnt her story of being lost and of not knowing where or how to find her parents.

"What's the matter little girl?" I asked her.

"I can't find Mum and Dad," she replied.

"What's your name?"

I can't be sure of her exact answer though it did have a distinct "Shar" sound, like "Charlotte" or "Sharmaine".

"I was sick," she said, "and when I got better my mother and father had gone. I don't know what happened to them."

"Where was the last time you saw them?" I thought that from the way she was talking, they'd also died on the station's grounds.

"Standing over there," she said, pointing to the entry door. "I went to sleep and when I woke up, they were gone. I've been looking for them ever since."

I began to understand what must have happened. This child had been brought to the hospital with an illness that had ultimately taken her life. Her parents had been to visit her, leaving by the ward's door – they'd probably given her a wave goodbye, too. After this she'd, "gone to sleep", probably a literal sleep in which she'd have physically died. Then she's woken in the spirit realm, but not realising that she's now dead, she's perhaps continued to see the ward and the people within it as it was before her death.

In other words, things hadn't changed for her: it was still the same place and she was still a patient there. It was only *after* that day of her parents' last visit that it would have seemed to her that they had stopped coming to the hospital. I dare say that for them, her death meant that they no longer needed to return to see her. She would not have known this, of course, and over the years she's waited for them to come back.

It's what is often called a 'limbo state', where the person doesn't realise that their physical body is dead and they continue to 'live' as normal.

It was clear to us that we needed to help this child and I began mentally calling for her parents, asking my own guides to help them come to us, too. Others of our tour group also surrounded us, lending their support of love and positive energies, willing the Higher levels to assist in this child's spiritual rescue.

Soon enough her mother appeared and then her father. There was a brilliant bright light appearing between these parents and their daughter as they were reconnecting with each other. It was wonderful, joyous and I saw the mother take Charlotte's tiny left hand in hers and the father took his daughter's tiny right hand in his. Then gently, the family faded in the light, crossing their beautiful, sweet girl into their spiritual world.

The three of us knew when she'd gone: we felt it and smiled to each other, uplifted to know we'd been a part of a very special experience. Lauren had caught up with me many months later, talking about this spirit child. She had put some research in to see if she could find any matching information and told me that a girl of this name and historic era was recorded* in the hospital's patients' lists, (although her death is unknown). It may well be that the child of this book was the same little girl we'd helped that night!

*An excerpt from the book, *In Quartantined*, by Lady Jean Duncan Foley, has reference to the following: "ex *North Briton*, 14-12-1839", this is the name of the ship she arrived on, and, "Charlotte Fuller, 2, (o) 31-1-1840."

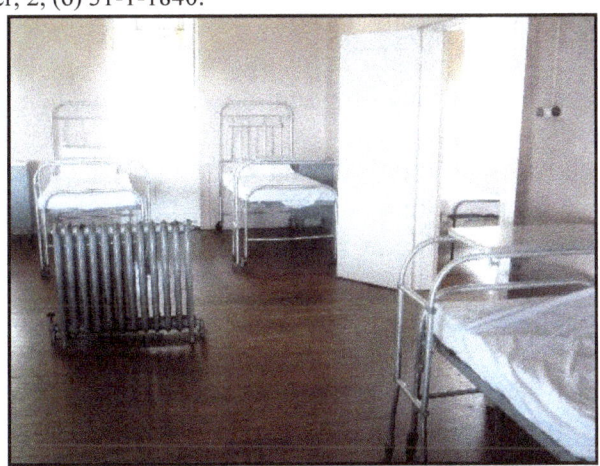

*Inside the hospital ward of Q Station.
We stood just in the centre floorspace between
the heater and door with "Charlotte"*

୧ଓଔଷ

For more information about the Quarantine Station at Manly's North Head, please see www.qstation.com.au

The Coloured 'Hearse'

One day my husband was working outside in the front garden. While pulling up weeds he noticed a maroon-coloured hearse driving slowly up our street. He thought it was an unusual colour, for he didn't think these cars came in this shade, yet to him, it did distinctly look like a hearse. Clive went on working when he decided to look up to see which house it was going to.

Our street ends in a cul-de-sac, yet the car had disappeared. He didn't know if it had since gone into someone's driveway, though on checking them, no 'hearse' nor maroon coloured vehicle could be seen. He now began to wonder if he had indeed seen any car!

"Is there such a thing as maroon-coloured hearses?" he asked when he came in for his morning coffee about an hour later.

I pondered on the question and realised that I hadn't recalled ever seeing a hearse in any other colour but white or black.

"No, I don't think so," I replied.

"Hm," was Clive's simple response, though clearly, he was still troubled.

As I tuned in for some understanding, I began to realise he'd had a premonition, especially as the car seemed to have vanished within minutes of seeing it. So I told him this.

"I feel very strongly that you may have had a premonition, and that someone may be about to pass over."

"Do you think so?" he asked, with his eyebrows raised. Clive wasn't unaccustomed to experiencing 'funny' moments so he was more curious than anything else. "How do you mean?"

"I know there's white and black ones, but I've never seen a maroon one. Maybe you'll hear of someone passing over in our street. Or maybe you should rest up and don't work so hard?" I thought maybe he will hear of his brother going to hospital, or perhaps one of our neighbours might take ill, or even die.

I wondered if I should worry about his health, or put it out of my head in the hopes he was okay. After a while, I decided to dismiss it.

That evening I rang Veronica, a medium friend of ours, to have a chat and mentioned Clive's vision to her, to see what she could make of it.

"How's his health?" she asked.

"Fine at the moment, I think." I then briefed her of my own interpretation of Clive's 'hearse'.

"Would it mean that we may hear of someone in our street going to hospital, or worse, hearing of someone dying?"

"No, I don't think so!" she cried. "I think the colour of the car represents his blood and that he's not well, or that there's something wrong with his blood. Maybe it's his veins or circulation. But I do think that he should go to the doctor for a check-up because it doesn't sound too good, seeing as how it was him who saw the hearse. Get him to ask the doctor to check his blood. I feel there is something wrong with his condition and it needs attention very soon."

A few days later Clive went to see his doctor for a review on his prescriptions and to see what tablets, if any, needed changing. When the doctor took his blood pressure he was shocked and confused and ordered a cardiograph to be done immediately. The results showed a blockage in one or two of his arteries, which needed immediate treatment.

He ended up in hospital within the week with an operation for two stents being placed into his badly-deteriorated arteries. He was lucky to have been in the right place at the right time to receive the treatment. I feel that if it wasn't for his personal vision of the maroon hearse and my conversation with Veronica that night, he may well have not been here with me today. Thank goodness for premonitions!

༄༅

Rob's Dad

During December on a holiday to my son in Perth, on the first night after we had arrived, Kevin received a phone call from a friend. I was sitting on the lounge, watching T.V. with the family, with Kevin seated at his computer just behind me.

"Hello Rob!" he said, answering the call.

Straight away I knew this was the friend Kevin had told me about in a previous conversation; Rob's house was haunted by a spirit and he was duly terrified of it.

After a moment, Kevin said, "Yeah?" with surprise in his voice. "The orbs are back"?

As Rob spoke some more, Kevin gave me a light tap on the shoulder to get my attention.

"Well, *I* can't," Kevin replied excitedly, "but I know someone who can! I have just the person in mind. My Mum just happens to be visiting us at the moment and if anyone can help you, she can!"

I had met Rob on a previous visit to my son, not for spiritual or ghostly reasons, but simply because he had come to Kevin's house while I was there. Back then, Rob happened to live a few doors' down the street from Kevin, but has since moved to a new house. So he was overjoyed to discover that I was into 'that sort of thing'. Kevin handed me the phone.

"Hi, what's up?" I asked.

"I've got orbs showing up around the place – you know orbs – they're supposed to be the lights of spirits, or ghosts. You know what I mean?"

"Yes," I replied. "I know what you mean. I've heard of them before but have never seen them with my own eyes."

"Oh, good," he said, as if reassured he wasn't talking to someone who thought he was a nutter. Mind you – you *never* laugh at a person who tells you of their unusual or paranormal experiences, not, at least, if they're serious. These people honestly feel that their encounter is real, and finding a way to describe it without being thought of as being stupid can be quite daunting for them.

"I've been seeing them on and off over the past few weeks," Rob said. "At first I wasn't frightened, since they didn't seem to want to harm me... *I* thought. Then they went away, 'cos I didn't see them for a while. But now there's one back and it's freaking me out!"

"Why's that?" I asked, curious, because I'd never heard of spirit lights ever truly threatening anyone.

"It seems like it's going around the rooms as though it's looking for something, or like it's trying to get my attention. I don't know who or what it is, or if it's trying to hurt me!"

Mentally I tried focusing on his home, even though I had not been there before, hoping I could see someone attached to them. I started to see these orbs floating around the room (a bit like dust) and one came towards me with the face of a man in it, wearing a sort of trilby hat.

"Has your father passed away?" I asked.

"Yes," he replied.

All of a sudden, the vision of this man showed him to be tall and thin with whitish-grey hair, which I relayed to Rob.

"Wow!" he exclaimed, "Now you're freaking me out! That sounds like my Dad! What's he wearing?"

I concentrated a bit more and then said, "Okay, it looks like a suit."

"Could you describe it?" he asked excitedly. "Is it a long one or a short one?"

I concentrated on the man a bit harder.

"A short, beige one," I said, looking at the spirit-man in my mind.

Rob seemed to hesitate for a few minutes before saying, "Does it look like a safari suit?"

I looked back at the man.

"Yes," I answered.

Rob was flabbergasted.

"Then why is he scaring the hell outta' me like this?" he demanded.

I looked back at the father. I could see that the calmness of his face was telling me that he wasn't meaning to scare his son. He didn't strike me as being a scary person, either.

"I don't think he wants to scare you," I explained. "He just wants you to acknowledge that he is there with you, and possibly has a message for you."

Then I observed the father brushing cobwebs from dusty shelves and walls with a feather duster, as if a room had manifested around him and it needed cleaning. When I explained this to Rob, he couldn't understand what this image of his father meant – until I asked about another person related to him. I sensed an elderly lady of average build standing in the same room as the man.

"Has your mother passed over yet?"

"No... not yet. Why?" he answered, sounding shocked.

I asked him if she was very ill, because seeing her there prompted me to think that she *had* already passed away. However, I didn't get that far.

"But she *is* in a nursing home with Alzheimer's," he quickly added.

That's when I realised his father really did have a message for his son – he was getting ready for Rob's mother to 'arrive' into the spirit realm, the 'cleaning away of cobwebs' was a symbolic reference of preparation. He wanted Rob to know that her time here on earth was getting close to her joining him in spirit, and he was waiting for her. Gently I explained this to him.

"You are not to worry," I went on. "Dad is getting ready for Mum, as he is telling me she has between three to six months here. Then he will be back to help her over."

"Ah, Sh#t! Sh#t! Sh#t!" Rob rapidly exclaimed. "I must go and see her! I'll go this Sunday!"

I'm not someone who swears yet I found his reaction quite humorous.

"Sh#t!" he repeated more quietly.

Poor Rob. I had thrown him into a panic and it didn't make me feel any better to know that I had travelled from one side of Australia to the other to tell him this sort of news. He was a friend in need of help – not someone who wanted to hear his Mum's death was looming on the horizon. We finished the call by arranging for Rob to come over to Kevin's house while I was still there. I had hoped to give him some comfort with any further messages or that he could at least find life a little easier to handle if he felt some sort of peace when going to visit his Mum the next time he saw her.

This phone call took place on a Thursday evening; Rob called around on the Saturday, and Sunday he visited his Mum in the nursing home. One week later (while I was still staying with Kevin), around ten-thirty at night, I went off to bed not thinking about Rob or his family. But this was to be no ordinary night.

The air was *very* warm, for the summer of that year in Perth was exceptionally hot, regularly around forty, to forty-four degrees (Celsius) over consecutive days! A ceiling fan in our bedroom gave us a little relief but nevertheless, I was tired and looking forward to going to sleep. However, Rob's Dad had other ideas…

He came to me as before, through my mind, saying he was pleased I had spoken with Rob and had told him that his Dad was with him. He now wanted me to tell him about a house he had built in readiness for his Mum's arrival. I had been blown away with how incredible it all looked.

The vision he showed me was exceptionally beautiful and the colours, quite vibrant. He had put in a lot of attention to detail. The home was a pretty, English-style country cottage of yellowish coloured brick and reddish roof tiling, much like terracotta tiles. There were small, square windows with bevelled glass panels, a garden filled with lots of colourful flowers, especially yellow roses, and there were hedges around the sides of the yard. Lining the front of the property was a yellow brick wall with mission-brown picket fencing in between its brick posts. He sat a statue in the middle of the garden path, that led to the front door, while a large water fountain stood on the left of this front lawn and a beautiful birdbath stood on the right side.

"Tell Robbie that this is what his Mum would want," the father said.

I got the feeling that this man was devoted to his wife and was aiming to please her any way he could. He'd even included a vegetable patch in the left-hand corner of the backyard! He thought of everything, even the flowers that surrounded the house and the bushes lining the perimeter of the property.

"Tell Robbie that I will be waiting for Mum," he said. "And when her time comes, I will take her straight to this home until she adjusts, before meeting the rest of the family."

"Of course," I mentally agreed; it was a wonderful place to go and his love for her was great.

"I'm so pleased that Robbie has an open mind to it all," he said, "unlike his brothers, who just shun it all out of their minds. I'm so proud of him! Tell him he's not to worry about the future, for I'm going to stay with him and look after him. And when it's Mum's time to go, don't cry sadness for her, but be happy for her that we're now together again. So if he feels like crying, then cry for joy that now his Mum will be out of her pain and suffering, and every chance they get, he'll bring Mum back to visit with him."

He had so much to say, but the hours, for me, were ticking by. I looked at the clock – it was three a.m. No wonder I felt extremely tired! I had to ask Rob's Dad to let me go to sleep as I needed my rest. I promised to write his story the next day.

He apologised for keeping me awake, for he wasn't caught up with time passing in the spirit realm. Happy for me to follow up with things later, he faded away. A few days on, I relayed everything to Rob, who verified much of it.

"Dad would have done all this," he said, smiling. "Did you know Dad was a self-made builder, and loved making things for Mum?"

I had drawn a rough sketch of the layout to show him.

"The house we had when I was younger *did* have a veggie patch in the back garden on the left-hand side," he said, confirming the details. "And the fence was styled like that and was the same colour, too. Dad loved to feed the birds – he'd be proud of his birdbath!"

He suddenly remembered an incident involving the roses.

"And yes, we did have yellow roses!" he said excitedly, "When I was a teenager, I was playing around one day with my brother and fell out of the bedroom window backwards – straight onto them! Dad was furious, for not only had I squashed the bed of roses, but he had to cut more of them away from me so he could pull out the thorns!"

"Well, he said," I began, repeating his Dad's message, "Tell Robbie that I'll be waiting for your Mum."

"Dad called me Robbie most of the time while I was growing up," he said, smiling. "Not Rob, or Robert or Bob, but Robbie. This is a photo of him and Mum together," he said, showing me the picture. They made a beautiful couple. Straight away I picked up that they were a devoted pair.

"They were devoted to each other, those two," he added.

As I looked at his father, I saw a captain's hat 'appear' on his head. I sensed that deep down, this man may have secretly wanted to join the navy but had never told anyone, or he may have been in the navy in a past life.

"Tell me," I asked him, "was your Dad ever in the Navy? I can see a captain's hat on him, as though he's on a ship."

Rob gasped.

"Oh my god!" he said, quite stunned. "You're unreal! No, Dad was never a captain in the Navy, but he used to wear that hat everywhere he went, whether it was the pub or the shops: it never left his head. Now I wear it from time to time."

I was just as thrilled, for this was the now third photograph I'd seen in which details about the person readily came to me. I quietly sent a big "thank you" to my guides and angels and especially Lydia, whom I am sure was helping me with this reading.

Rob very happy, and very amazement with it all.

We had hoped to catch up again before Clive and I returned home to NSW. I was keen to see how he was getting along, but unfortunately, he was unable to visit with us, though he did call to give me his regards.

I wished him well.

Within the year, Rob's mum did pass away, but hopefully he's drawn comfort from his Dad's message about the cottage.

The Friends I've had to Farewell

Soon after my first book went to the publishers, the promise of my spiritual gifts returning has come true, but it has been a slow journey. In the early days, spirits would appear only faintly, often as outlines, or shapes, or with only a part of themselves slightly visible. But it has been enough to give me courage to go on. I know that I must work very hard to achieve and respect this precious gift – my Gift of Seeing Spirits.

I know my gifts are really coming back pretty strongly, too, for whenever I attend funerals, I can see the people who have just passed over. Usually I see them walking around the coffin or around their relatives, both indoors or outside, including the gardens.

Avril's Husband

In the space of three years I went to four funerals, including my niece, Tina's. In November, a year before Tina's death, I went to Western Australia to visit my son and his family again. One of my dearest friends, Avril, and her husband, Peter, lives quite a few suburbs away from him, and Clive and I wanted to visit them while over there. We've known each other for many years and we get on very well together, especially over a cuppa. But one month before leaving home for this trip, we were talking with Avril on the phone, telling her of our holiday plans.

"That's wonderful dear," Avril said, "we'd love to see you again. But I must warn you, Peter's not well. He's contracted cancer and it has spread around his body."

We were devastated. This wonderful man, kind, gentle and softly-spoken, was terminally ill. I couldn't wait to get over there.

When we arrived at Kevin's house, we soon rang Avril to see how she and Peter were going, hoping that there was good news and that he might have improved.

"Sorry Love," she said sadly, "He's in hospital now, very ill and he possibly won't last very long."

"Oh Avril," I said, feeling awful, "I am so sorry to hear it. What hospital is he in? We'd like to see him as soon as possible please."

"You'd better not visit, my Love. You don't want to see him the way he is now," Avril said. Her heart meant well, for she was worried we'd be shocked by his physical change, as cancer, sadly, robs the body of all its strength. But we would not be daunted – these were and are very dear people to us.

"But we don't mind! We know he won't look well," I added, eager to see him before it was too late.

"I'm sorry Love, he's just too sick to see anyone just yet. Could you perhaps wait a few more days?"

So rather anxiously, we waited a few more days until we were given the okay to visit him. On the third day we got the call to say we could go in. I jumped for joy, because I really feared we would miss him. His health was so poor that all visits were strictly limited, and though we were with him for only about an hour, our chance to say goodbye was precious.

Peter was so happy to see us, too. Within minutes he asked if we could sit in the waiting room with him instead of at his bedside. A nurse was called and came into his room, requesting us to leave while she and some other staff helped him into the wheelchair. Despite the difficulty and toll on his energy to move, he came out and sat with us.

He persevered under the circumstances, though we could plainly see that he quickly tired. Knowing he needed rest, we decided to leave, hoping to see him again before we flew back home. Sadly, this didn't happen.

Avril spoke to me a little while afterwards, saying that Peter had asked her if we'd really been there.

"Was that Joyce and Clive come to see me earlier?" she relayed, quoting him.

"Yes," she'd answered. "That was them."

"I thought I was dreaming," was his reply, for he knew we lived on the opposite side of the country and that to have come that distance was for him, both a miracle and a joy.

But, within that first week – two days following our visit – he passed away.

While at the funeral I saw him. He walked up to Avril and stroked her hair, then touched his children on their shoulders as though he was saying his goodbyes to them. And then he walked back to the coffin, seemingly pleased with how he now felt: he wasn't in any more pain. I, too, could feel this sense of perfect relaxation inside of me, as if I were picking up on his new health.

It was incredible.

My younger son, Kevin, also attending the service, saw Peter by the coffin, smiling at us as it lowered into the chapel's platform floor. Then gently, he faded away.

At the wake at his home, I saw him briefly again, sitting in his favourite chair. Again, he softly faded, and I feel so blessed to have seen him not once, but twice that day, knowing he was – and is – at peace. Our love to you, Peter.

৸◌৪

Joan

In February 2013 came the third funeral. It was for Joan, a beautiful lady and lovely friend who, as with Peter, died of cancer – and of all days, Valentine's Day. A week followed until her lovely, moving service, where she was buried among stunning gardens at a local cemetery.

She, too, stood near her husband and towards the end of the service, then moved to the side of the white coffin. She was looking down at it as it lowered into the earth.

"It's a beautiful coffin, thank you," she was saying. "And such beautiful flowers!" She looked at her loved ones – so many of us there. "But I am not in it!" she said. "I am here! That is only my body-suit and I am not in any more pain!"

She saw me watching her and smiled, then also faded quietly away.

I was extremely thrilled to see her looking very happy and a lot healthier. I know that she, too, is at peace.

༄༅

Alison

A month later came the passing of another friend's mother. Zena was an elderly lady who had fallen and broken her hip a few months earlier. She hadn't fully recovered from the operation and went in and out of hospital a few times, checking herself out on the last visit and returning to her home that she shared with her daughter, Alison, and her family.

She passed away that same night or in the early hours of the next morning.

At her funeral I saw her stroking the flowers on her coffin and walking around her family, looking at them. She went over to some people seated on my side of the room, just out of my sight, then back to the coffin with a brown walking stick in her right hand. I thought this was unusual as I had never seen her with a walking stick before.

She also went up to a baby in its pram, near one of her grandchildren, to stroke it, but the infant cried. Apparently, Zena had woken it out of its sleep. It was rather comical to watch her hurry back to the coffin, presumably hoping the baby would go back to sleep, or at least quieten down. But its mother had to take it outside.

After the service I managed to ask Alison if her Mum had had a walking stick, much like the one Alison was using herself.

"Yes," she replied, "It was just like this one, only brown."

Aside from the sadness of the occasion, I was pleased of what I'd seen, convinced now that my dream of seeing spirits again was finally coming true for me.

It was interesting to hear a few weeks later, when speaking with the family, that one of the grandchildren, then of around sixteen years of age and who lived in the same house where Zena had died, would hear the woman's cough every night at midnight when she was going to bed. They have assumed it may have been the time when Zena had passed over, and that she was trying to tell her granddaughter this, for it's only her that has heard it.

Fortunately, none of the family are frightened by this, knowing Zena is at peace and means them no harm. It's also her way of saying her goodbyes.

༄༅

"Mike" not "Mark"

Early in March 2013, I had a phone call from a lady whom I had met in the previous month at our local markets. Louise wanted me to give her, and her daughter, Skye, a reading. Skye had just flown in from Adelaide, South Australia, and was staying with her parents for about two weeks before returning back to her home. So it was arranged for me to visit them three days later.

Mediums and psychics want to give their clients the 'perfect' read, but as we don't necessarily hear spirits' voices, or perhaps can't hear them clearly, it is very hard if the person you are reading for cannot identify the spirit(s) who are trying to come through. I read for the mother first and all went well, then when reading for Skye, I saw a young man standing directly in front of me. When he spoke, it sounded to me like he said, "Hi, I'm Mark," or, "Mork,"; it was hard to understand him because it seemed muffled. "Tell her I am here," he added.

"I have a young man standing just here," I said, indicating the place, "and he is saying the name of Mark, or Mork, but he's showing me the letter 'M'. Do you know him or would he be related to you, for I feel he was close to you?"

"No, sorry," she replied.

"Well, he is just standing there and won't go away, so think of the name and maybe you will remember him before I have finished with your reading."

I continued on with her reading, informing her of a move very soon, still feeling very frustrated that she could not recall this man, who remained there the whole time.

"Are there any questions you want answered?" I asked, nearing the end of our session. "I will try to answer them for you if I can."

"No, I think you have answered all of my questions," Skye said, "except I was hoping that my brother might have come through."

"Okay, hang on, I'll try," I replied. "What is his name?"

"Mike," she said.

That's when the 'bombshell' dropped on me like a ton of bricks. I nearly cried.

"Mike," I repeated. "Then this spirit who won't go away is smiling, so this must be him." He sounded funny to me and this was why I couldn't understand what he was saying. Because spirits sometimes tend to speak softly, you don't always understand what they are saying, and sometimes they mumble. In this case, the spirit I saw did both: he must have been saying "Mike" in a strange, deep voice that had sounded like "Mark".

On explaining this to her, Louise obviously realised the possibility of this being the case.

"Yes, he did speak funny, with a deep voice," she cried.

"Then I'm happy he came through for you both," I said.

"Tell them I am fine," Mike added.

I passed this on and we chatted a little more about him. I was so relieved once the air of confusion had been cleared and both ladies were delighted with their readings.

"He's pleased that you now know he's okay," I finished, as the conversation came to an end.

By the time I was leaving, I was feeling elated at having given successful, positive messages to people in need.

ಏಡ

Guided by my Beautiful Late Son

My book was now finally in the hands of the publisher and we were ready to plan for a launch. It had been a long enough journey to this point and I was both excited and anxious to see this project finally coming together. This was around mid-March 2013.

I had the urge to ring a lady in a nearby town, ten minutes away, to enquire about her healing centre. I felt the need for healing and I also wanted to go to a meditation circle. We made the booking to see a lovely lady, called Sheree, for the following week.

She gave me a very good healing session and while talking with her, I happened to mention that my one desire was to have, or belong to, a Spiritual Church.

"Look no further," she said, smiling, "for the lady who now owns this place is doing it up and will not only be having a meditation circle, but plans to have a Spiritual Church in the big hall. Did you see it when you came in?"

"No," I replied, blown away. "I came in through this door." This was a rear entrance to the building and quite close to the room where we sat.

"I'll go and get her. If she is not too busy renovating this place I will introduce you to her."

This brightened my day.

The new owner was very excited to meet me when Sheree had told her of my interests. She wanted to read my book straight away but she also had to get back to her work.

"Why don't you borrow this book that Joyce has given me?" Sheree suggested. "Then you can see if you'd like to sell them in your shop."

The following week I caught up with this lady and asked her how she found my book.

"Oh, very good!" she replied enthusiastically. "I love it! I've just finished reading about your late son. It was so horrible! So sad! I would like to put it in my shop when it's up and open to the public."

I was dumbfounded; I guess I wasn't expecting such an enthusiastic response.

"I can relate to your experience," she continued. "My son died two years ago in a bad car accident. Everyone loved him. They miss him terribly and were shocked that he'd died. Like you, I know when my son is around because when we sit outside on the back veranda the light flickers frequently."

We arranged to visit again the following week.

It was here when we realised that my son's spirit had brought us together by guiding me to Sheree, who then introduced me to the lady, and that *her* late son had also guided her and her husband to this building.

"I'm also looking for people who can read cards," she had added.

"I can do that!" I promptly replied. "I use plain deck cards. They're my 'bible'. I was taught many years ago when I was in my thirties by my aunty."

"Oh good!" she exclaimed. "Well, let's see what you're like. You can give me and my good friend a reading, how about that?"

A few days later, in one of the spare rooms, I sat down with the lady and, unsurprisingly, brought through her son. He was very cheeky but funny and kept interrupting the reading, which made her laugh. He assured her he was fine and very happy.

Her good friend also enjoyed a positive reading with me and afterwards, both women asked me to read for their sons later in the week. The new owner's younger son liked his reading, in which I told him he would get a job real soon. The following week I met him again and he confirmed to me that he'd gotten the job he was going for. He was over the moon, and was also very touched that his big brother had come through for him.

ೞ⚬ಐ

Strange Coincidences

Three days later, I went to a local haberdashery shop to find some material to make new curtains. I got talking with a lady who worked there.

"Do you need some help?" she asked.

"Yes," I said, and told her what I was looking for.

"Go upstairs to the curtain department," she suggested. "You might find something there close to what you're wanting."

I did and soon found what I needed. On my way back down the stairs, I noticed the lady in the same area where I had first seen her. In my excitement of my upcoming book launch, I felt compelled to call out to her to let her know I'd found something suitable.

So I made my way over to her and struck up a conversation, showing her the fabric I'd picked and explaining how it was also going to be used at the launch. This led to telling her about the book, the Gifts I used to have, and as to how and why I'd lost them.

"Oh," she said, "is that when you started to see spirits, after your son died?"

"Oh no," I replied. "That started when I was ten years old." I showed her a copy of my brand-new book, which I was so proud of and now carried with me in case I met people who were interested in hearing about it.

While we talked, I noticed a young spirit man standing to her left, but I didn't say anything. I briefed her of my stories including my son's, because his was so significant to where I was now at. I told how upset I was not to have been able to see him since he'd died.

"But I always know when he's around for I can smell his aftershave," I said, "and quite often I will feel his arms around me when I feel down and depressed."

"Oh!" she gasped sharply, throwing her hands up to her face as her eyes filled with tears. "I know the feeling! I often get arms around me too!"

"Have you got a young man that's passed over?"

"Yes, my son passed over a couple of years ago."

"I'm sorry if I've upset you," I said, feeling bad.

"No," she assured. "That's why I understand what you're saying, because after he'd died, I smelled and felt the same things. But I didn't know what to do about it!"

"Well, I believe he's standing right next to you," I gently added, pointing to her left. He gave me a grateful smile.

"Really?" she asked, surprised. Her eyes lit up and she looked to her left.

I described the young man's features to her.

"Yes, that's him," she said, smiling.

"When you smell him, or feel arms around you, that's him, trying to let you know he's around," I explained.

She seemed to calm on hearing this.

A bunch of flowers appeared in his hands and he started to say something else.

"Hang on," I said to her, "He says, "give Mum these flowers". He wants me to give you these yellow flowers," I explained. "They look a bit like daffodils, but I'm not sure. They are a vibrant yellow and they are in a cluster. He said that he can't give them to you himself as you wouldn't feel him giving them to you, but you would take them from me."

She clasped her face again and said, "He loved yellow roses!" The tears filled her eyes.

"He said that the yellow flowers are for peace," I went on, repeating his message. "He wants you to be at peace and not to feel guilty about anything, as he is also at peace and very happy where he is."

This poor lady was beside herself and didn't know how to thank me. I started to put my book away and was about to say my goodbye, when I heard him call out to me again.

"Tell Mum I'm teaching little kids over here, and not to worry about me, and that I will always be with her whenever I can!"

I passed on the message.

She threw her hands back up to her face.

"I can't believe it!" she cried. "When he was alive, he always wanted to teach little children when he was old enough!"

"Well don't worry, for he's doing it now and is extremely happy," I said, smiling. On an urge from her sin, I walked closer to her. "He wants me to give you a cuddle from *him*," I said, reaching forward. "This is not from me."

She accepted the hug with a smile.

"Thank you," she said, "and funny… that is exactly the way he used to hug me. He always gave me a tight hug just like that!"

"That's probably because he was with me while I hugged you."

"I'll try real hard to come to your book launch!" she added. "If I can get time off work."

I left the shop feeling quite happy, hoping I'd given her some comfort. I sent a big "thank you" to all the angels and spirits for allowing me to see her son and share his message with her. It confirmed, for me, that I was most certainly getting my former gifts back – as well as my confidence!

༺༻

Elsie

My first official book launch in April 2013 was exciting. Of the people there who came to see me was a lady by the name of Elsie, whom I had first met about two years ago when she played the narrator in a pantomime of *Cinderella*. She had come up to my local area to spend a couple of weeks with her close friend, Heather, who was attending my book launch at the same time.

Before the launch had officially started, Heather and Elsie were there, eager to meet me. While we chatted, I was immediately drawn to the presence of a lady who was standing next to Elsie.

"Has your Mum passed over?" I politely asked.

She looked at me with a funny expression, though she also seemed impressed.

"Yes, but that was a long time ago."

"It doesn't matter," I explained, "because she is here and has asked me to tell you to slow down, for you are doing too much, and if you don't look after yourself, you will burn out. So don't take on too many roles and cut down on the plays asked of you."

Heather prodded Elsie's shoulder. "See, I told you so," she said, grinning.

I turned to Heather, having gained the strong sense that she, too, was also over-working herself.

"And you are also doing too much and must look after yourself too!"

Heather looked stunned, yet both women had a good chuckle.

After the launch itself and answering the questions some of my audience had asked, I took time to talk with people individually. Whilst chatting with one person, I happened to glance at my daughter, Christine, who was there helping me with the event. She was busy writing something in my diary and had Elsie and Heather with her. Soon she came over to me to confirm if the date she'd booked was alright for me to give them both readings.

It turned out that Heather's granddaughter, who had also come to the launch, wanted a reading as well, but she was due to return to Sydney the next day. We arranged for me to come out to Heather's home that very afternoon for the granddaughter, and then I'd return in a week for both Heather and Elsie.

On the drive there I prayed for an accurate reading and at the door, who should be the first to greet me but Elsie. I felt honoured by her wonderful, enthusiastic attention. She made me feel special in a way that I hadn't felt before. They took me to a small room where the granddaughter promptly closed the door behind us. I suspect she didn't want the others to hear what we discussed. Thankfully I did not disappoint her and indeed, helped put her mind at ease for a problem that she was facing. I was pleased and as often happens at the end of these sessions, she gave me a big hug.

Afterward, I chatted briefly with Heather and Elsie of their upcoming readings, suggesting to them that, if they'd like, my daughter Christine could read for one and I, the other.

"That's a brilliant idea!" they said. "That way it would only be an hour instead of two hours!"

"Do you have a preference for which one of us reads for who?" I checked.

"No, we don't mind! Just so long as we both get a reading!"

Later that night, my sister, Hilda, rang me to apologise for missing the launch. She knew Elsie through the theatre, too.

"That's alright," I said. "It's a long journey for you to make." I then briefed her about my encounter with Elsie's Mum, who had said her daughter needed to slow down.

"Wow," said Hilda, listening with interest. "That makes sense. You know Elsie has recently had a heart attack?"

No, I didn't know. Nor had Elsie breathed a word of it. I now understood why her mother had given her that warning – she had to slow down or she was in serious danger of damaging her health further!

When the day came around, Christine and I asked the ladies which of us they would like to have read for them.

Neither could make up their minds and we joked a little to ease any concerns.

"Why don't we do what we do at the markets?" Christine asked. "Let them look at the card decks and choose which set they're drawn to?"

The ladies were more than happy to try.

Christine took out each of our respective card decks and started placing them on a table. She hadn't got far – only managing three – when Elsie saw the next set.

"Oh dragons!" she quickly said and with a chirpy smile, added, "I love dragons! They'll do! Whichever one owns them can read for me please!"

Christine and I smiled at each other.

"Okay Christine, it looks like you get Elsie and I get Heather," I said.

We chuckled a bit more about how eager Elsie was for her reading and the two left for another room.

I sat down with Heather and after getting her to shuffle the cards, I studied them quietly. I did not like what I saw and I did not quite know how to tackle it.

"There's an upcoming death I see for you," I began, and pointing to the respective card, I added, "there is a death card here, but there is no picture card to say who it is, so I feel you will only hear of it; possibly within a two, which could be two weeks or two months, even two years. But my feelings are saying two weeks."

"Could it be my husband, as he is not a well man?" she asked.

I concentrated on this card, (the Ace of Spades, upside-down).

"No, it's definitely not your husband," I said reassuringly. "Even though there is no picture card, I feel it's more of a female around you. My senses tell me it's possibly someone you know, such as a close neighbour or a friend."

I then said what I now rather wish I had not.

"For example, just say – and I don't mean this literally – it could be Elsie. Do you understand? You will only hear of it. Sure it will make you sad with whoever it is, but it is *not* family related."

I think this settled her down, though I didn't realise just how strong my senses were.

"For me to be more accurate, I would need to have either a Jack, a Queen or even a King's card on the left of the Death card to say if it's a male or female, so you will only hear of it. Or if it's on the right of the Ace, it would say that someone has already passed over. But this has neither one to say who it is. All I can go on is my inner feelings."

By now I felt that I had said enough and went on with the rest of her reading. When I ended, the phone rang. It was her husband, wanting Heather to go and pick him up from their son's place about five minutes away. She insisted that I make myself comfortable while I waited for my daughter to finish with Elsie, because she herself wouldn't be very long.

So I proceeded to pack up my cards and wait, then very shortly I heard the door of the other room open. '*Great timing,*' I thought, assuming Christine was now finished and also ready to leave. But I was wrong.

Christine wasn't quite finished. She needed my help as Elsie had a question that my daughter felt was beyond her abilities to give a responsible answer on. She believed that I, with my years of experience, could better help this lovely, warm lady.

I sat down opposite Elsie.

"How can I help you?" I asked. "What do you want to know?"

With a quiver in her voice, she said, "I would like to know why my son took his own life."

I immediately felt quite uncomfortable, for this sounded like the question I used to ask clairvoyants regarding my own son, Arthur, in 1997, (as I had lost this precious gift in 1984). So I held my selenite heart in the palm of my hands and tried to concentrate on Elsie's son.

After a couple of minutes, I heard his voice.

"I was very depressed and didn't know what to do at the time," he said. Then he mentioned a man's name.

"Who is Darren?" I asked Elsie.

"That is my other son. Why?"

"Because he just said that Darren was not there for me."

"That's right," she replied, "he was in Melbourne at the time and was very upset when he got the news. But why was he depressed?"

"I feel that there was a lady involved, because apparently he had just broken up with her and this made him very upset, because he loved her. But she didn't want him anymore. I think there was someone else she loved more than him."

Elsie had a blank expression.

"I feel that because Darren was not near to him, he didn't know who to turn to, too. But he is very happy now and is sorry for what he did."

I looked up at her.

"He's around you and Darren quite a lot, especially when you are not well or feeling down."

Elsie seemed to settle a bit on hearing this. She was very pleased and grateful for what we had achieved for her.

Upon leaving the room we saw Heather and her husband sitting on the lounge. Heather introduced us to him and like with the others, I felt a need to give him a 'health warning'.

"You also have to take care of yourself. Don't do too much."

"Don't worry, I won't," he assured.

We smiled and made our way to the front door. I turned to Elsie without a second thought.

"Next time you visit Heather, get in touch with us and we'll have you all come to our place for a cuppa."

Smiling, she said, "Okay, you're on!"

Then we left, not realising just how soon I would 'see' her again. While driving home from Heather's, Christine told me how she'd found reading for Elsie had been difficult, and she needed some feedback.

"I had a lot of trouble trying to get anything for her!" she said with anguish. "I picked up the 'Beaver in her'. I knew it meant she was hard-working – which she confirmed. But I really struggled to see much else!"

"I know from a man I read for a while ago that I could get nothing from the picture," she explained. "It didn't matter how I looked at it or what I asked, I just felt like I was looking at a picture, there was nothing I could sense from it that related to him. It was later that afternoon when he confessed to me that he was a sceptic. That's when I knew why I was getting nothing on him.

But with Elsie, that wasn't the case! I *could* sense stuff, just very little stuff!"

There was very little I could say, not knowing what the cards were, much less how to read her decks. Nearly two weeks passed when the answer became a bit obvious to us.

༄༅

Christine and I were helping with the regional Eisteddfod at our Entertainment Centre within the fortnight of seeing Heather and Elsie. Late one particular afternoon, my job of selling tickets had finished and now I sat in the side wing of the stage, helping my daughter as she managed the competitors for their performances. While we waited for the adjudicator's results, my gaze rested on the empty stage.

There was Elsie and Hilda tap-dancing together, having a wonderful time!

Christine came back off the stage a moment later and stood next to me.

"I can just imagine Elsie and Aunty Hilda out there together," I whispered "They'd have a ball of a time!" But I couldn't shake thoughts of Elsie's from my mind.

At that very moment Christine's mobile phone started quietly buzzing.

"Hang on a minute," she said, reaching into her pocket. "I've just got a text."

She read it through, and frowned. "Oh," she said, bending closer to whisper in my ear. "Elsie's died."

I was shocked; my mouth dropped open.

"But I just saw her on the stage!"

"Michelle just sent me the message," she said, handing me the phone:

"Elsie died this morning and was found on her kitchen floor. They think that she had had a massive heart attack."

Chills ran down my spine.

It was the last thing we expected to hear and the news upset us for the rest of that day. I was stunned, and I think this was why I couldn't let go of her image. Christine had to return to the microphone and I looked at the stage again. Elsie's son was beside her, giving her a great big hug. Instantly I knew that she was happy and that what I saw was her way of saying goodbye to me. Her mother appeared – the same lady who had stood beside Elsie at my launch. They hugged too. Then her father also appeared with her. The reunion was so joyful.

Elsie had been very strong around me in the time since she passed to the time I have written about her here. She has asked me to tell you this story for her. Most of it has been her wording.

So I say to her now, "Thank you for coming to visit me even though it is from Spirit. I will never forget you."

I have often felt her presence around me, and I am grateful for having known her.

Elsie

The WWI Soldier

Things were starting to look up for me, for I was being asked to do more readings for people. It was my first real break that proved to me Lydia was keeping her promise of Spirit returning my Gifts. I felt I had been rewarded and accepted back into the spirits' world; I was now starting to feel whole again – and certainly blessed. Since this time, I have gotten stronger with my Gift of seeing my beautiful spirit friends.

I was asked to read for an elderly lady who lived not too far from my home. I usually go to the client's house or, if this is not suitable, I have taken to hiring a private study-room in my local library. She explained that her husband wouldn't agree with me being at her house, for he didn't believe in this sort of thing, so we made a date for the local library.

While reading for her, I saw a man appear in the corner of the room. He was standing very straight, with his hands firmly resting in front of his stomach, and he seemed to be studying me while also keeping an eye on the lady. I wasn't going to frighten her, though I wondered who he might have been.

"I see a man wearing a uniform, or a suit of some kind. He looks regimental; he's wearing medals on his chest and he stands there very straight. Do you think you might know who it may be?"

"It sounds like my great grandfather," she said, "who died in the First World War when I was very young."

I moved on when I saw the name 'Peter' appear in front of me and, sensing it was her husband, I felt he was also under some kind of stress.

"Is your husband's name Peter?" I asked.

"Yes," she confirmed, "but he's not dead."

"Yes, that's right," I replied, "I know he's not dead, the feeling is so strong. How is his health going? I feel he is under a lot of stress?"

"Not too good," she replied.

"He needs to relax a bit more," I said.

"Yes, that's very true," she agreed, "because we are trying to sell the house. He wants to stay in the area and I want to move away from it to be closer to my family, but he doesn't know which way to go and this is causing him a lot of stress. We also don't know if we will have enough money to move. And he doesn't want to leave his friends."

"Well, the cards indicate that you *will* move and that everything will be alright, whichever way you go. And the man in the corner has said not to worry, things will work out for the better."

Before we finished I focused back on the man in the corner of the room, who had stayed there all along.

'*Is there anything more I can say to this woman?*' I mentally asked him.

He turned sideways to show me the wings on his back, then held out a beautiful bunch of red roses for her. '*I am her great grandfather and her guardian angel,*' he said.

"The man in the corner says he is your great grandfather and guardian angel, and he is looking after you."

"Really?" she asked, smiling.

"Yes, and he is handing you a beautiful bunch of red roses – these are his love for you."

"Oh, thank you," she replied, as tears filled her eyes and flowed down her cheeks.

We finished the reading on a high note, and I left knowing she had been comforted.

Months later, I learned that she and her husband had moved house and the stress he had been under was gone as they were both quite happy with their new surroundings.

༺༻

Red Roses, for love

Pictures Can Tell A Thousand Words

After my book had come out, I was asked to go to another lady's home, whose daughter, Diane, had bought a copy for her. Diane had already had a taste of my abilities when she met me and so had told her mother, Patsy, about me. Both ladies attended this session together, in which a great deal of information came through.

As I was finishing Patsy's reading, she asked if I could see anyone [in spirit], which is a common thing that people ask me. As I looked around the room, I glimpsed a few silhouettes and shadows sitting in the lounge area to my right, among them, a tall, handsome man appearing very strongly in the corner, near an indoor plant of some kind.

"There is a tall, handsome man in the corner over there," I explained. "He's wearing a big hat and has a walking stick in his right hand."

Patsy appeared to be very surprised and put her head in her hands. "Sh#t!" she said. "That sounds like my father!"

Then I saw the spirit of a lady in the kitchen, facing us, holding a plate of pikelets.

"I see a lady over there, she has a plate of pikelets in her hands and she is saying that she hasn't had time to make the cream yet."

Patsy cupped the sides of her head. "Oh no! That'd be right," she cried. "It sounds just like Mum! Every time we went to visit her, she would have a plate of pikelets and we had to whip up the cream. Her excuse was that we'd turned up too soon and she did not have time to make it. She loved cooking pikelets!"

Diane called out to her spirit grandmother, "The jam is in the fridge!" and gave a little chuckle.

Patsy then got up and brought a photograph over to me, which showed a man and woman together. "Are these the people you can see?" she asked.

"Yes, that's the man I can see over there in the corner," I replied, pointing to the spirit man by the plant. "And that's the lady in the kitchen."

"That's my Mum and Dad," she explained.

"Oh, gee, he's nice looking," I commented, for he looked exactly like the man I saw in the corner.

"My father died thirty-six years ago," Patsy said, "and Mum went fifty years ago."

Then, for the first time in my life, I felt compelled to touch the picture with my index and middle fingers. I didn't even know why I was touching it – it was like someone had picked up my hand and put it there.

But something strange happened when I did this, something that, in all of my years of reading, I had never experienced before. I suddenly saw a lot of land around him – not the actual background of the photograph – and there were tables loaded with fruit and eggs on them.

"Was your father a farmer?" I asked, feeling excited. "Because I can see a lot of land around him with tables full of fruit and eggs on them."

"Yes!" she gasped. "Dad was a fruit farmer and supplied the whole of this town!"

Tingles raced over me – for what I had seen was true.

"Can you see anything with Mum?" she asked, also thrilled.

I touched my fingers to the image of her mother, instantly seeing four women appear in a line in front of the parents, and one young man standing between the

Mum and Dad. I told her what I saw and where they were in the photo.

"Did your Mum have four girls and one boy?" I asked.

"No, Mum had four girls," she replied, "and two boys."

"Well one of them is not in this photo, so he must have passed over?"

"Yes," she answered.

"Then he must be with your parents," I said, meaning it literally. "Because he's not in this photo, as I can only see the ones that are still living."

Diane was sitting there smiling, later explaining that she'd never known her grandparents – they'd passed over before Diane was born. Then Patsy blew me away with another photo she brought over, one showing four adult women – the same four faces that had appeared in the parent's photograph.

"These are my sisters, two of them are twins," she said, smiling gleefully and handing it across to me. "Can you pick which ones they are?"

Eager for the challenge, I glanced over the photograph, not seeing any resemblance of identical faces with any of them. However, after touching my fingers to the first lady on the left of the frame, I picked up what I felt were health issues related to her.

Patsy confirmed the results.

I continued scanning the picture, looking at the next woman standing beside the first one, and sensing the warmth of her personality coming through.

"I feel that this one," I said, pointing to the specific individual, "is very easy to talk to, and if you had a problem you could always talk to her and she would listen. She's like a counsellor, who will comfort you and guide you in whatever the problem is."

"That's right! She would!" Patsy exclaimed.

I moved on to the third woman, feeling for anything that might indicate something about her.

'That's the twin to the first one,' I heard Patsy's mother in spirit say.

"Is this the twin to this sister?" I asked Patsy, pointing to the first woman.

Patsy turned to her daughter with a big grin on her face.

"She's got it right!" she said excitedly. "Not many people do! How could you tell?"

"Your mother just told me," I replied.

"Really? That'd be right! Trust Mum to give it away!" she laughed.

The fourth face was, of course, a younger version of Patsy. With a grin, I said, "But I don't know anything about this one…"

We all laughed at the joke. Yet a third photograph was given to me, this one of Patsy's son, (still living, who we'll call John). I studied it for a little while.

"He's not happy," I began. "I sense that he's in, or has been in, a bad relationship."

"Yes, that's right," said Patsy, nodding. "She's not a very nice girl. She treated him very badly."

"Right, well, it seems to me that they're going to break up, or that they already have, and he's also going to move interstate."

"Well, you're right, Joyce," she said, looking a bit grim. "They did break up a while ago and he's still quite upset about it. And the new job he's got is interstate!"

This was encouraging, as it was confirming to me how strong I was in reading pictures.

"From what I can see," I went on, "this son will find another lady, and he'll be very happy with her. I sense it might be say, about six to eight months away yet, but I think I can also see a child with them too."

Patsy's face lit up.

"Oh, really? Are you sure? I'd like that!"

"Well, that's what they're showing me here," I replied. "And according to this, the new job is much better, too! He'll be happier there."

She showed me a photograph of her husband, which I gently touched, too.

"I can see a lot of pigeons around him," I said.

"Yes, he's a bird breeder. That's why he's not here today. He's away in the city looking at a particular pigeon to buy."

"I can feel he's got a hip problem," I went on, "and he's got a lot of aches and pains up and down his legs."

"Yes, he does," she confirmed.

"Just tell him to watch his health," I urged, feeling slightly concerned; it was not life-threatening, but I knew Patsy would want some direction or answers in addressing the situation. "It might be time for him to get his health checked out with the doctor."

Finally Diane handed me a picture of a dear girlfriend she'd known but who had since passed away. I honestly do not remember what I sensed with this picture, other than this woman was now no longer in pain and was very happy in her spiritual world. Though still sad at her loss and missing her deeply, Diane was satisfied with the messages that came through for her from this woman.

Both mother and daughter were very pleased with their readings – which had been scheduled for only an hour each but which had gone for longer than planned due to the surprising new Gift of reading the photographs.

"Dad supplied the whole of this town!"

On finally leaving them, Patsy turned to me and said, "Of all the clairvoyants that I've been to, none of them have ever brought in both of my parents. Mum had always stayed 'behind' my Dad. But you, Joyce, have brought both of them through *together* – at the same time! Thank you!"

I was on a high, for this was an experience with a huge bonus. Spirit was watching over me, they had allowed my original gifts to return and though I felt they were coming back slower than I wished for, here I had been given a *new* one!

Patsy ended up buying another copy of my book to give to her brother who lived interstate, as she knew the brother would enjoy it as much as she did.

༄༅

Beautiful Spirits

The Mother in the Wheelchair

The very next day after having seen the father with his fruit in Patsy's photograph, I went to another lady's home. Her name is Janelle and she had also bought copies of my book a month earlier, for both herself and her friends. We chatted for a while when she explained that she was expecting a girlfriend called Lisa to pop in for a few minutes before going on to work.

Once Lisa arrived and we were introduced, I began to feel that this lady needed a quick reading, because I sensed a deep sadness around her. After the two spoke for a while I felt compelled to say something about it.

"Are you having trouble with a male child?" I asked her.

She looked at me quite funny and said, "Yes. How did you know?"

"I just felt a young male presence around you and that this child is experiencing some behavioural issues, like severe mood swings and hyperactivity that requires the help of a professional therapist, for he seems to be emotionally unpredictable.

Although she was blown away with my psychic insight, she was also reserved in how to take action on the situation.

"I've been confused about that," she said. "I have tried to understand him but I just get abuse from him whenever I've brought in help! I don't know which way to deal with it!"

Beautiful Spirits

"I think you should take him to someone who understands his type of condition," I said.

She mentioned a doctor's name, saying, "She's a very stern woman and very disciplined. But she might be a bit too strict for him."

"No," I replied, again sensing the appropriateness of this professional doctor coming into the son's life. "He needs that sort of discipline. She will be very good for him."

Lisa – who did not come to Janelle's place for a reading but who had inadvertently received one – was taken aback, seemingly impressed with my accuracy.

She said she would look into the matter as soon as she could and eventually left us to go to work, as planned.

"I'm very happy for you telling her that," Janelle said afterward.

"Oh that's alright. I just say what I feel – what the spirits tell me. I knew something was wrong with a young male around her – who I sensed was her son, and that she was having difficulty in dealing with it. The messages I received were what she obviously needed to hear."

"We've tried telling her, too," said Janelle. "Her other friends and I have all told her how to handle the problem, but she didn't seem to take our advice. Now that you have said almost exactly the same thing, I feel she will act on it this time."

Pleased, and still excited from the successful photo readings of the day before, I mentioned my newest Gift to Janelle.

"Really?" she said, glowing with excitement. "I'd like to see that!"

We went into the kitchen then and officially began her card reading, in which her father came through. Afterward, she brought me a photograph of him with his wife beside him and, thankfully, it happened again.

Essentially, seeing his face in the picture merely confirmed the visual image I had received of him in Janelle's card reading. However, it was the lady who came through with a specific message for her daughter.

Janelle's mother showed me herself sitting quite calmly in a wheelchair, a condition that felt, to me, very confined.

"Was your mum in a wheelchair before she passed over?" I asked her.

"Yes, she was, poor thing."

"Well she doesn't need it now," I said. "She's showing me her legs are straight now, and that she doesn't need the chair. She's well again and can walk without any pain."

"Oh God Love her!" Janelle cried, and tears filled her eyes. "I miss her so much."

"She wants you to know that they are both very happy and are with you, and both still love you, too," I relayed.

The mother gave me a very dainty smile – both her parents did, grateful for the opportunity to reconnect with their daughter. Janelle was overcome with emotion, pleased to learn that they were well, together in spirit, and still watching over her.

Janelle's Dad and Mum

By the time I was leaving her, I was feeling quite confident that I was now a lot stronger than before... my Gifts truly were coming back to me as promised!

༄༅

In early March, my youngest daughter, Christine, was asked to do a reading for the sister of Patsy (Diane's mother, see chapter, *Pictures Can Tell a Thousand Words*). I had not met her sister, but I recognised her from the photo that Patsy had shown me before.

Christine used an available back room of a local shop, while Patsy and I went and sat in seats near some big windows down the front. There, she showed me another photo of her daughter, Diane, and it included Diane's husband, too. They were holding their infant son.

Diane's brother, (Patsy's living son, 'John'), was also in this picture. As I glanced over the photo, five other people appeared there, including a small child. These were their relatives, now in spirit. I pointed to the areas of the picture where I saw them standing.

"I can see lots of people with them," I began.

"Oh yes?" said Patsy, quite interested.

"Mmm. There's two lots of grandparents here," I said, pointing to them. "I feel that one of them is your Mum and Dad."

She understood right away, nodding with an agreeable sound.

"And there's another lady that I feel may be your mother's Mum   your grandmother," I added.

"Oh really? That's nice to know. Thank you very much."

"In the front here," I said, pointing to a place in front of John, "there's this little girl with long black hair. She looks to be about seven or eight and I feel she may have been a child of his that he may have lost at about this time."

"Yes! You're right!" she cried. "His ex-wife miscarried around seven or eight years ago!"

"Right, well, I get the feeling from her that she is looking after Diane's baby son and will be his guardian angel throughout his life."

"Oh really? Isn't that lovely?" She was thrilled to hear the news and was smiling from ear to ear. "Speaking of John, do you remember telling me he'd find a new woman? And that he'd like his new job?"

"Yes," I said, recalling the conversation.

"Well, he has found a girlfriend! And she's lovely, Joyce! They've hit it off so well that they're thinking of getting married!"

"Well!" I said, surprised and happy for her. "Congratulations! I'm so happy to hear it. I told you he would!"

"And he loves his job, too! It's so much better than the old one. He gets a lot out if it."

I was thrilled, too, to know what an incredible new gift I had gained since returning to this spiritual path. The afternoon was lovely after that as I could hardly keep my feet on the ground with joy.

Much, much later down the track, on talking with her over the phone, Patsy told me that John and his partner did get married and that they were trying to start a family together. Diane had moved up the coast and had since had another son, and Patsy had also relocated with her husband to be with her.

༄༅

Beautiful Spirits

The Broadmeadow Exhibition

Martin's Mate

In late August, I attended the annual Model Railway exhibition at Broadmeadows, near Newcastle, of the New South Wales Hunter Valley region. It was a strange weekend as things turned out, with lots of interesting people there. Each year, on the Saturday night, the organiser holds a dinner at the local club for the exhibitors and crew.

After returning from our dinner, I was met at the gates of the exhibition by a young man in his early twenties, who was there to let us back in to the grounds of the venue, where many of us slept.

We'd hardly walked past him when he asked, "Are you Joyce?"

"Yes," I replied. "Why?"

"Do you do the readings?"

"Well I try to," I replied, not wanting to boast. "Who told you I could do readings?"

"Kerryn did," he said, smiling shyly. "I'm Martin. I'm a member of the club."

I knew the lady he spoke of. She is a good friend of ours, too and she and her husband have a trade stand at most of the exhibitions I go to.

"Could you please give me a reading tonight?" he politely asked.

I looked at the time, it was getting late and I really just wanted to go to bed. The night wind was freezing. I was tired and getting colder by the moment.

"Oh I don't know," I began, about to suggest we catch up in the morning. But it was not to be, as a young man quietly appeared beside him, and he seemed eager for us to talk right now.

"Go on," he said to me from his spiritual plane: Martin had no idea he was there. "He desperately needs a reading. I will help you."

"Okay," I said, perhaps a bit reluctantly. "Just give me ten minutes to wash up and I'll see you in the dining area."

Martin was very excited and couldn't thank me enough.

I made myself a cup of tea and set up a table for his reading. When I was almost ready to start, Martin arrived.

I briefed him as to how I worked with spirits and he seemed to understand.

"I believe in this stuff," he said, eagerly waiting for me to start. But what he didn't know was the big surprise in store for him.

Before I picked up the cards, the young spirit man who I had seen at the gate appeared beside Martin again, so I decided to begin with him.

"Do you have a friend that passed over? I feel this was a young man who you possibly knew at school and who may have been a good or best friend."

He sat back in his chair, looking stunned and as though he was thinking, *'how do you know that?'* He took a few minutes to answer.

"Yes... he was in an accident." Martin didn't say what kind of accident it was, but that didn't matter to me because his spirit-friend told me what had happened to him. He showed me a wrecked car at an intersection.

"Was he in a car accident?" I asked Martin, at the same time that Martin was starting to say the same thing.

"He was in a c-" He stopped and, looking shocked, said, "Yes..."

"Mm," I said. "He's standing to your left side and he's telling me what had happened." But the spirit man began showing me two different seats of the same car. "Now he is confusing me," I went on. "He is showing me two different seats. First he shows me the back seat, then the front seat. Was he in the front seat and thrown into the back seat?"

"Yes, he was!"

"He wasn't driving the car, was he?" I asked.

"No."

"Your friend said the driver was drunk," I added. "The young man is not telling me his name but I feel that it's a small name like... 'cat' or 'dog'." I struggled to find a good example and added, "Or 'Mike' or 'Mark'. It's something simple. Not a long name like 'Raphael' or 'Mathew'. All I can see is a small white space."

"His name was Sam!" Martin suddenly piped up.

"Right, well, Sam's telling me he's okay now. His passing was relatively quick. I feel that he died there, in the back seat."

"Yes, the Ambo's couldn't save him. He was already dead by the time they got to him." He was still affected by the trauma, it seemed.

I was pleased I'd gotten the size of his name right and that I could pass on Sam's message to him. Picking up the cards, I decided to move on. "Right, now to read your cards."

I showed him what to do with shuffling the pack and splitting them into three piles. He had a short reading but it was great and he was very happy with it. Most of all, he'd had his eyes opened to the existence of other side through Sam's presence. I'm sure he really did believe in spirits beforehand, and now it was confirmed for him.

ಬಂಗ

Kerryn's Cats

The next day Kerryn came to see me. Christine, my daughter, was with us and while we were talking to Kerryn and another lady, I picked up on a ginger coloured cat walking around her. Then a black and white cat appeared beside her.

"Did you have a ginger cat and a black and white one that's passed over?" I asked her.

"Yes," she replied, looking surprised. "The ginger one was run over by a car in front of our house, and the black and white one fretted for her mate and died a few months later. But I feel them around me all of the time." Kerryn turned enthusiastically to the other lady. "My husband has seen them running up and down our hall sometimes and ends up yelling at them to cut it out – and they stop and all goes quiet!"

"Yes, well I can see them with you now," I said, pointing down at her legs. "And I can see that they also visit you on the bed-"

"Yes! I can feel them walking up and down my bed of a night time," she cut in excitedly, "and when they get as far as my shoulders I just say, "Go down to the bottom of the bed!" and they do!"

Christine must have been tuning in too, for she said,

"I can also see one of them outside in the backyard. It's sort of like, I'm looking through a top-storey window; or it's on some tiles of a lower roof."

"Yes, that'd be the ginger one – she loved to sit out on the roof of the back room in the sun of a morning. But the black and white one loved sleeping on my bed," Kerryn added. "When we go out I leave a mohair rug folded up on the bottom of my bed for her, and when I come back, there's an indentation where she has been lying! So I know they're always with me."

"Well, we didn't know anything about them, did we Mum?" Christine said, looking at me. "So I guess you've got further proof?"

"Oh yes! I miss them terribly!"

She was so happy to have shared that conversation with us, to learn that what she regularly experienced at home was, in fact, confirmed to her by us. Every time she saw us after that, she smiled wonderfully with joy.

༺༻

Roses for A Dad's Daughter

Just after lunch time an elderly couple came up to my stall and saw copies of my book on display. After quickly looking through one, the lady asked me if I did private readings.

"Yes," I answered. Then the inevitable was asked.

"Can you see anyone with me now?"

Nearly everyone I meet, who learns of my clairvoyance, asks me that. Naturally, I could see him standing beside her.

"Yes," I replied, "You brought a man in with you, who I feel may be your father."

The lady's husband turned and walked away, as though to say, "Oh no, not again." She seemed to ignore him, perhaps too used to his reaction.

"The man is on your left side," I added, pointing to her left shoulder, "and there's a lady to your right," also pointing there. "Have your parents passed over?"

She looked surprised but pleased that I could see them.

"Yes," she said, nodding and smiling. A tear also began filling her eyes.

"Is my father happy?" she asked.

"Yes," I said, seeing the smile on her Dad's face. "You were very close to him, weren't you?"

She nodded again. "Out of all the children, I was the oldest and Dad and I got on very well. He used to say that I was his favourite."

"I thought so," I replied, "because he is standing very close to you." I looked at the spirit-mother. She held kids' jumpers in her arms, as if showing me that she'd made them. "Mum did a lot of knitting, didn't she?"

"Oh yes, when the children were little. But we were not as close as Dad and I."

"Mum says she's sorry she was not always there for you as she was caught up with other children's needs at the time."

The elderly lady nodded, saying nothing but listening to her mother's message of apology.

Then next I saw her father digging in a flower patch.

"Was your Dad a gardener?"

She nearly flipped. "Yes! He loved his garden!"

"I thought so, because he's giving you a big bunch of red roses mixed with Baby's Breath."

She gasped, and tears filled her eyes.

"Oh, he grew red roses and they were his pride and joy!" she cried with a quiver in her voice.

"Well if you can accept them, this is his way of saying he is still around, and they are for love. He is giving you a lot of love. In fact, if ever you smell roses around you when there are no flowers in sight, this is his way of letting you know that he is around you, and that he is watching over you."

The lady was so pleased I had given her this information. She took an order form that had my contact details and folded it, putting it in her pocket with a smile.

"I'll definitely be in touch with you," she whispered, before walking away.

The rest of the day went well. I felt great that I had done my best for Spirit over the weekend in helping them connect with their earthly loved ones. We get closure from these moments, and also comfort: it's wonderful to be an important part of that. This weekend showed me even more how my clairvoyant strengths are finally back, and very strongly now.

༄༅

"Mum's Here"

Late in June, 2013, my husband and I were invited to see the medium, Lisa Williams on stage, in Newcastle, N.S.W. We arrived a couple of hours early and decided to find a restaurant or take away for a meal, as it would be reasonably late when the show would finish.

On walking down from the theatre where Ms. Williams was to perform in, I saw a dark-skinned lady following us some twenty metres behind. We'll call her Marie. I was hoping she was a local, who could tell us where we could find a nice place to eat, so we stopped and waited for her to catch up to us. When she was close enough, I gave her a friendly wave.

"Excuse me," I politely asked, "are you a local here?"

She smiled and replied, "No. I'm from Queensland. I've just flown in a couple of hours ago and am now looking for somewhere to eat."

"Oh, same here," I said. "We're here to see the Lisa Williams show. We've just arrived and are looking for somewhere to eat, too. I was hoping you'd have been able to tell us where a nice place is."

"You're going to that too?" she exclaimed. "So am I! Unfortunately I don't know my way around this place, and I don't want to stray too far from my hotel room for fear of getting lost!"

We laughed at the seeming coincidence. But of course, Spirit seldom uses 'coincidences'.

"What if I stick close to you and we find somewhere together?" she suggested.

"Sounds like a great idea," we agreed.

About ninety metres off, around the corner, we found a university café which appeared to suit our needs.

We settled down at a table and prepared to look at the menu. Then a small, chubby-looking Aboriginal lady, in spirit, appeared to the left of Marie.

"Tell her I'm here," the spirit-woman said.

All I wanted right then was some soup and to relax, not a conversation between loved ones in spirit and those here on earth. Mentally I spoke back to her.

'No, I want to have my soup,' I gently explained. *'Besides, I don't know her enough and I don't want to freak her out while she's eating.'*

Our food arrived and happily I tucked in. The spirit-lady stood there the whole time, not being a nuisance, just patiently waiting.

The three of us chatted about the upcoming show, eagerly discussing what we wanted to get out of it.

"I'm hoping my late son will come through," I said, and briefly described his passing.

"I suppose I don't mind if I don't get a reading," said Marie, "I'd really like to meet Lisa though."

"But wouldn't you like someone from the spirit world to come through?" I asked, trying not to 'see' the lady beside her.

"Oh well, it'll be nice if it does happen," Marie agreed, "but I suppose I'm not *too* fussed if it doesn't happen, really. I believe Lisa is a really nice person!"

The ghostly lady wanted to be heard.

"Go on, tell her I'm here. Tell her, "Mum's here"."

"Ahh… has your mother passed over?" I hesitantly asked at last.

"Yes! Why?" she said, slightly startled.

"Because she's been begging me to tell you that she is standing there, and I didn't want to freak you out while you were eating. And besides, you might get a reading from Lisa and I don't want to influence you."

She smiled knowingly. "Oh, I wouldn't freak out, because I find this fascinating," she replied chirpily. "Can you see people too?"

"Yes," I said, feeling relieved and happy that she was comfortable with the subject. "I've even written a book about it."

I rummaged around in my bag for a card that had my name and a picture of my book on it. "She's been waiting all of this time since we sat down to talk to you," I added, speaking of Marie's mother.

"Oh really? Thank you!"

"Yes," I went on. "And is Mum on the short side?"

"Yes," she answered.

"And a bit chubby?" I didn't want to sound rude, however it *was* how this lady appeared.

"Yes," said Marie again.

"And has she got shoulder-length, black, curly hair?"

"Yes, she does – or did."

"Well that's how she's looking to me, here," I said. "And she wants me to say "Hi" to you, and to tell you she loves you."

Marie sort of turned side-on, addressing the mother she couldn't see. "Oh, hi!" she said, a little strangely. "Thanks Mum."

While we chatted on about her, I saw her father, in spirit, walk past on her right side and I also felt there was an older man with a walking stick around. I told her about these men, too.

"I can understand my father being here," she said, thoughtfully, "but I don't know who the man with the stick is."

"Don't worry right now," I said encouragingly, "but when you go home, ask your relatives if they can help you. Someone may know who it may be. Who knows, you may get a better reading from Lisa?"

I wasn't about to assume I was any better than a professional in this field.

"Thank you so much," she said, her smile beaming. "I'll get in touch with you in the next few months, when I find out who it might be!" As we prepared to leave for the theatre, she added, "I think it's amusing that I came here to see one medium and then saw another one! I've even had a meal with you at that!"

"Oh well, things often happen like that," I said, grinning too.

She turned to Clive sitting next to me. "It must be freaky knowing your wife can see people who have passed over. How do you deal with it?"

"I read tea leaves," he said in his dry-witted way.

"Yeah, it doesn't worry him," I smartly cut in, "he believes in the afterlife!"

"Wow! How about that!?" she smiled. "I came to see one medium and now I'm sitting with *two*! This is great!"

Strictly speaking, my husband isn't a medium, nor has he ever claimed to be one.

We walked back to the theatre and parted company to change for the evening show. We saw her briefly on her return but as we were seated elsewhere, we missed catching up with her again that night. We met Lisa Williams after her performance and also got a picture with her as well. I just *had* to take a photo of my late son with me, hoping she might draw something from it. She signed the photo, but we didn't receive any messages from Spirit through her.

I don't recall that Marie got a reading during the show, but I did get to see her have her photo taken with Lisa, too. It was clear she was over the moon with joy and that her trip down from Queensland was worthwhile. If nothing else, I was obviously meant to go to this event, even if it was only to meet this lovely lady in the street and reconnect her parents with her in the café. I certainly hope to meet her again in the future.

ಲಿಂಕ್

The Spirit of a Living Baby

In the second week of July I attended the local markets with my giftware and crafts. I also took my cards in case anyone wanted a reading. I had set my stall up at around 6:00 a.m. and finished at about 9:30 a.m. and had just sat down to have my breakfast when my first customer walked in. The next hour went slowly, with only a few customers, and then a crowd seemed to appear from nowhere.

It was cold to begin with, as it was winter and at around mid-morning I was chilled and frustrated, for not many people were actually buying – just looking and walking on. Then my spirits lifted.

A lady walked up to me. "Who does the readings?" she asked.

"I do," I replied, momentarily taken by surprise. "My daughter usually comes with me and we both do readings, but today I am on my own. So if I have any customers, you will have to excuse me while I attend to them. But I will come straight back to you!"

Well, luck was on my side. She accepted the situation and asked for a reading anyway. Thankfully only one customer came along at the time, paying with the right sum of money, so I wasn't held up with finding change.

The lady was very pleased with her messages and took my business card, saying she would be in touch with me later in the year. I was very happy now, for I had just made enough money to pay for the cost of my stall fee.

'If no one else comes along, I will pack up and go home early to a nice warm fire and some lunch!' I thought to myself. But Spirit had other ideas…

You see, within the next ten minutes the customers started arriving, steadily buying small items over the next half an hour. I think it must have been lunch time when I decided to start packing up. Barely half a dozen things had been put away when the crowd reappeared and I was busy looking after several customers. In a short break I sat down to catch my breath, when suddenly my world opened up again. Two lovely ladies walked in, asking me who did the readings.

'Wow!' I thought, thrilled that this mother and daughter were actually interested. *'This is really happening!'*

"I do," I replied, and told them about the potential interruptions that may arise as before.

The mother, (whom we'll call Nancy), agreed and went to the card table in the back of the stall, out of the way of people passing by. Her daughter followed her, wheeling in her baby in its stroller.

As soon as Nancy sat down, I saw another spirit-lady appear beside her, on the left. Mentally I asked who she was.

"Her mother," said the spirit.

"Your mother," I began, "has she passed over?"

She looked at me surprised. "Yes, a long time ago."

I nodded. "Yes, because she has just told me so. She is standing right there," I said, pointing to her left shoulder. I continued to pass on the spirit-mother's message. "She said you are not to worry about a problem that you have. Can you identify with this?"

"Yes," she said, smiling.

"She said everything will be alright and you just have to take things easy, for she said that you are taking on too much. Do you worry about other people?"

"Quite often I do!" Nancy answered. "I like to help them wherever I can."

"Well, Mum said to ease up because you will only burn yourself out," I went on, "and she will be with you as much as possible, and she is with you every step of the way."

I then went on to read her cards; her father came through from Spirit though he didn't have much to say; I saw another, younger, man who also kept very quiet. Then the ten of diamonds turned up next to the jack of spades, telling me that a young man had drowned.

"Do you know anyone who drowned?" I asked. "I feel it was a young man."

Instantly tears filled her eyes.

"Yes," she said, "my brother. He was on a navy ship in the war and it got bombed and sank. My brother went into the water and drowned. I was very young at the time of his death."

The younger spirit-man confirmed it was him.

"Well, I have him here and he said he is alright now and he watches over you. Also, he loves you very much and is proud of you for what you are doing."

I then noticed a third, much older man, appear on her right, alongside of the first man.

"Is your husband still alive?" I asked.

"No," Nancy answered, "He died a long time ago."

"Okay, because I can see a third man just there. He has his hand on your shoulder."

"Could this be him, my husband?"

I described his looks.

"Yes, that sounds like him!" she said. She seemed to feel good at hearing of these people still being with her. As the reading progressed I became aware of many spirits around her and I couldn't help but say something about them all.

"My, you have a lot of people on the other side, haven't you?"

She nodded softly. "Yes."

But time was getting away from us for me to bring them all through to her, though I knew she was very happy by the end of the session. She couldn't stop thanking me and as she stood to leave, her daughter, (whom we'll call Rebecca) came to stand beside her.

"Would you like a reading too?" Nancy asked her.

"Yes, if that's okay," Rebecca said excitedly.

Well, I thought I was only going to give the mother a reading, but it turned out that both of them wanted one! Of course, I couldn't refuse; we sat down and I prepared the cards for her. While shuffling the deck, Rebecca turned the baby's stroller in, slightly facing towards me. Until this point I hadn't seen the infant and now my attention was drawn to a sweet young spirit girl standing beside it, who looked to be of about three or four years old. I'll call her Angela, since this spirit looked a bit like an angel with her long blonde hair and her short white dress.

Angela desperately wanted to be heard.

"I'm here! I'm here!" she kept saying.

At first I took it to be that Angela was the spirit of a child whom Rebecca had lost, so I said, "Have you lost a baby, or maybe a small child, or have you had a miscarriage?"

"No, this is my only baby," she said.

"It's just that I have this beautiful little girl – just here, standing beside the stroller. She's saying, "I'm here! I'm here!" and I don't know why. Hopefully she will tell me more during the reading," I added.

"My baby is a little girl," Rebecca commented helpfully.

The baby seemed to have a big smile on her face, which at first, I thought, was due to wind.

"I'm here!" Angela repeated.

I concentrated on the spirit, knowing there was a strong reason for her presence here. *'Are you a little baby that's passed over?'* I mentally asked.

"No," she answered.

'Well, what relation are you to the baby? Are you her guardian angel?' I persisted.

"I'm her spirit until she's old enough to talk to the family," she said. "Because babies can't talk to adults."

At last I understood the connection, bearing in mind that Angela was all of three or four – she didn't have the communication skills to properly speak her thoughts.

"When she's old enough," Angela went on, "I'll go into the baby's body and 'take over' from there."

It made sense, and I explained all of this to Rebecca.

"Tell Mummy," Angela said, "when I get older I want to be a dancer and gymnast, and I will be very good at them!"

I was flabbergasted. I relayed the message and noticed the baby smiling each time I spoke of the spirit-girl. It must not have been wind, after all.

"Thank you," said Angela.

The news seemed to please the young mother, too, and I suspect she will remember to enrol her little one into dancing classes once her daughter is old enough.

This experience gave me a great feeling; both of these two readings were very interesting, particularly as I hadn't spoken with the spirit of a living person before!

༄༅

An Interesting Telephone Call

One day a lady called Mary rang me to inquire about my abilities into seeing spirit people. She lived only a short distance away and she wondered where she could buy my book, for she couldn't find it in the local book shop. Someone had shown Mary their own copy that they'd bought directly from me and I explained why the local retailer couldn't stock it: being that it was published with the American company, Balboa, who had their own distributor (who, for some reason, didn't supply to Australian book shops).

"I have copies available," I explained. "I can meet you in town. Just say when it will suit you to catch up."

As we chatted, I could feel that not only did this lady need a reading, but that she was also feeling down. I began tuning into Mary's voice, as I had done in my earlier days way back in the '70's before I'd given my gifts away. I saw an elderly lady standing beside, and just a little behind, Mary's left shoulder. Her mouth was moving as though she was trying to speak to me but I couldn't fully make out her message. All that was apparent were the letters M-O-T-H-E-R.

"Has your mother had passed away?" I asked.

"No, why?" she replied.

"Has your grandmother on your mother's side passed away?" I asked.

"Yes," came her answer. "A long time ago when I was a young child. Why do you ask?"

"Well, I can see a lady standing next to you. She is elderly looking, her hair is greying – it's like she'd been black-haired, but it's now going grey and it looks a bit like the colour of steel wool. She is telling me your Mum's ill"

"Really?" said Mary, rather amazed.

"This used to be one of my Gifts that I lost," I explained to her. "Because my son's religious beliefs at the time said that what I could do was evil and wrong!"

"Oh isn't that terrible! What a dreadful shame, huh?"

"Yes, but I was promised by Spirit that I would receive these Gifts back when I finished writing my book," I explained. "I would get one for every story I wrote, and for taking the message of having Gifts – of keeping them and using them despite what people or religion might say – to the world. And this is what's happening!"

Seeing the spirit grandmother gave me greater confidence in my spirit friend, Lydia, that she was indeed keeping her promise to me. I was blown away with what I was getting.

"Now, is your mother ill?" I enquired. "And is she in a nursing home, for this lady is showing me an elderly lady in a wheel chair and a lot of beds around a room."

"Yes," Mary confirmed. "She has dementia and doesn't recognise me sometimes when I go to see her! Other times she does, and when we admitted her, she said that she didn't want to go into a nursing home." Her voiced dropped mischievously. "But we cheated by saying to her it was only for a short while, just until she got better, because we couldn't look after her the way these people can, which seemed to settle her down a bit."

I found myself nodding, as my own mother didn't want to go into a nursing home either and we had told her the same story.

"Mmm," I added, "and she doesn't appear to be very happy about it."

"But that was a year ago," Mary went on, "and I think she knows that she won't be coming out. This is possibly why she looks unhappy to you."

"When you go to see her, does she often smile at the wall and appear to go off to sleep for a short nap?" I asked. "And when she wakes up, is this when she recognises you?"

Mary gasped.

"Yes!" she cried excitedly. "How can you tell? It's as though you are there in the room with me!"

"Well, when your grandmother mouthed the word 'mother' to me, I realised she was trying to say that she was with your mother all the time, and she is waiting for when it's her time to take her over into Spirit – when your Mum's time is ready."

"Oh, okay," Mary replied thoughtfully.

"When you see her smiling at the wall, she is really looking at her Mum. It just looks like she's staring at the wall."

"Wow," said Mary, sounding captivated and also a little relieved.

"While she's napping," I went on, "she is being shown the Other Side briefly, so when her time comes she won't be frightened."

"Oh right... So they're sort of getting her ready?"

"Yes," I said, "And when she wakes up, she sees you and feels good. She possibly thinks you understand where she went!"

Mary was impressed that I could see all of this while talking to her on the telephone.

"Next time you go to see your Mum, let her know not only that you love her, but that it is okay if she wants to be with her Mum. You may see a dramatic change in her."

"Really?!" she exclaimed.

"Yes, and she will possibly go peacefully in her sleep sometime in the next few weeks. But this is *only* when her time will be right for *her*. More so," I added, concerned for any fears that Mary may have been feeling about her mother passing on, "her Mum will be waiting to take her over, and she will be out of her pain and suffering."

Mary thanked me for explaining this to her and felt that she now understood more of her Mum's mood swings. She made arrangements to see me later that week at her local coffee shop where she would get a personally signed copy of my book. I was so pleased at how our conversation had gone, for to communicate with Spirit in this way brought back that wonderful connection I had once so enjoyed.

ఏుఁ

Another Market

In the last weekend of September 2013, I went to another market to sell my goods. It's in a quaint, idyllic holiday area where a lot of people retire to for the peace and tranquillity that can be found there. But it can also get very busy when the tourists come to visit.

Usually I have a great day at these markets but this one seemed to be reasonably quiet. It was slow and I was starting to feel down. I knew that if I hadn't sold something by midday or done any readings, I would be out of pocket – for I still had the stall fee to be paid.

By around ten-thirty I was getting desperate. Although some giftware had sold, it wasn't near enough to cover the cost of the stall. I decided to quietly pray for things to get better. At about eleven, my first reading came along. This made me happy because, even if I didn't sell another thing that day, I now had enough for both the stall fee as well as some lunch.

After the reading was done, I thanked my angels and guides for sending the lady to me. I was preparing to begin the big pack-up when out of the blue, a few more customers stopped by and bought some things. It was enough incentive to make me stay a little while longer. I began to feel – quite strongly – that someone was watching over me. Then a dear lady arrived.

"Excuse me," she asked very nicely, "do you do readings?"

"Yes," I said, smiling. "Take a seat."

She did, and my emotions lifted. As she settled, I sent a silent message to Spirit.

'Thank you, Angels. Please stay with me and guide me through this lady's reading.'

Much to her surprise, everything I told her she could acknowledge.

Eventually I came to the Death card.

I try to avoid telling people they will hear of a death, or know of someone very close to them that is about to pass over, unless I get told by the spirit to say who it is. In this case, the person knew who had already passed over.

"Was there someone close to you who was very ill?" I began. "I feel this is a male figure, possibly a father or grandfather, and they have already passed over."

"Yes, my husband," she said, quite calmly and with a tear in her eye. "Could this be him?"

"Yes," I replied, feeling relieved. "I thought it may have been but I didn't want to upset you by saying it was him, in case of worrying you if I was wrong."

She gently nodded.

"I understand what you are saying," she replied.

"When he passed it was very quick, wasn't it?" I continued.

"Yes," she said with a soft voice. "He was only ill for a short while, then he was gone. He died a few months ago and I miss him so much."

"He's with you most of the time," I added, sensing his closeness to her.

"Yes, I feel him around me sometimes."

Then a lady's presence came to me, like that of a mother.

"Has your mother passed over as well?"

She sat back in her chair, seemingly surprised.

"Yes," she answered. "Is she here also?"

"Yes, but at the moment she is not saying anything, just observing me. I don't think she understands that I can see her." I waited a bit, hoping the mother would communicate a message for her daughter. "Come on Mum," I tried urging her, "say something. I won't bite you."

But the spirit-mother stayed very quiet, apparently preferring to listen to what I had to say. A few moments later I asked the daughter if she had any questions that she would like to ask of her mum before the session was over.

"Yes, could you ask her what to do with a problem I have?"

Now, as I have not got this lady's permission to disclose this part of her reading, I cannot reveal the question, nor the answer. But the mother did reply and her daughter was cheered immensely, saying, "Thank you, Mum. I needed to hear that."

Then I saw a garden.

"Who liked the garden?" I asked. "Did your husband or mother grow yellow flowers in the garden? Because someone has just given you some. I'm not sure if they were roses or daffodils, or some other flower, but they seem to be all mixed up in this bunch they're handing you."

She gasped with shock.

"Now that *is* strange," she said excitedly, "because I spoke to my sister recently, saying how much I missed Mum. And because Mum loved flowers, especially yellow ones, the other day I received a big bunch of mixed flowers from my sister, and they were all yellow! That's incredible!"

"If your sister wasn't aware that these would mean anything to you other than she was trying to cheer you up, then yes, that would be incredible. But it may have been your mum was with her at the time of her going shopping and put the suggestion into her head to get all yellow flowers for you, to let you know that she is at peace and wants you to be at peace."

But I could also sense her mother saying more.

"She wants you to take things a little easier," I gently said. "She says that you are taking on too much and not looking after your own health. I think she was trying to get the message to you that she was thinking of you at the same time you were thinking of her!"

The lady understood exactly what I was saying. She was very excited to know her mum was happy and still around her. She accepted everything I had given her in her reading and as she stood to leave, I found another lady waiting in line. The second lady sat down and I did her reading; when she stood to leave, a third lady approached my table.

Wow, from being bored and down with slow business, to being very busy – I had cheered up immensely.

These last two ladies knew each other. As the third lady took her seat, she said to me, "She's a beautiful lady. She's just lost her husband."

"I know," I replied, smiling. "I just brought him through for her."

Again, I am limited to what I can say of this third reading, for, although I have her late father's blessing to mention that he and the lady's grandparents came through, I did not get to ask her if she'd mind me including her in this book (it's not often I do ask).

Of course, she too missed her dad terribly, for she was his favourite daughter, saying that she could get away with anything with him when growing up. I know she accepted and also understood what I was able to give her. Just like the first lady, by the end of her session I saw yellow flowers pass by my face, going towards her. I felt they were coming from her dad.

"Did your father have a flower garden? Or did he like flowers? For I just saw some yellow flowers coming towards you."

She looked a bit surprised.

"These are for you," I gently added, "to have peace and to let you know that he is also at peace."

The lady almost cried.

"Dad had a flower garden," she began, with tears filling her eyes. "Mostly yellow roses, but also some mixed ones, too. He loved yellow flowers. Thank you, I needed to hear that."

ೲఴ

Yellow Roses, for peace

Kym

In the first week of February 2014, I went to another market, selling my craft and giftware and also doing readings for people. My first one went well, as did a few more, but while talking with a lady about some lace for sale, she happened to notice copies of my book on the table. She wasn't there for a reading, though she seemed interested in what she saw. Her name is Kym.

"Is this your book?" she asked.

"Yes, it is," I proudly replied and told her how I came to write it. "All of it is true! I used to be able to see spirits, many years ago. But my late son-" I said, pointing to his picture on the cover, "that's him there – he asked me to give it up."

"Oh, what?" she said, slightly frowning. "Why?"

"Because at the time, he was deeply religious, and he was told that what I did was evil."

"Oh no, really?"

While I talked with her, I started getting enormous chest pains. They hurt so much that I really thought I was having a very bad heart attack. But I didn't want to say anything in case I upset the lady, so I tried to finish the discussion as quickly as possible, with the idea of getting my husband to ring for an ambulance. I was so glad that he had come with me this particular day as usually he stayed at home.

"I'd like to buy a book," Kym said before the conversation was over, "but I don't have enough money on me."

"That's okay," I replied, "take this." I gave her my business card. "When you are ready, give me a ring on this number and I'll meet you somewhere. Or perhaps at the next market the following month you might see me?"

"Oh thank you!" she said, putting her hand to her mouth for, though she didn't say why, she looked very sad and her eyes were teary. "I'll definitely get in touch with you soon, because I believe what you are saying!"

She walked away to a small table not far from my stand to have a drink. I was on the verge of telling my husband to help me pack up because of the pain I had experienced, when I noticed it had completely gone! I thought about it, wondering if it had been indigestion, but it was too real and too painful to have been passed off that way. Confused, I looked over at the lady again. She was talking with her husband, wiping her face as though wiping tears away.

I felt compelled to go to her, to put my right hand on her left shoulder. I 'knew' what had caused my pain. I walked up to her and politely caught her attention.

"Excuse me for being rude," I began, "but do you suffer with chest pains?"

She gasped.

"Yes I do! Why?" she cried.

"While we were talking," I gently began, "I felt enormous pain in my chest. It was so bad that I thought I was having a heart attack."

"Oh really!" she exclaimed.

"Yes. But when you left, my pains disappeared."

"That sounds right!" she said. "See, I understood what you were saying, because when we lost our daughter in 2001, I was very down."

"Did your daughter go over with chest problems?"

"She'd had a heart defect," said Kym, with tears filling her eyes again, "and she was in a lot of pain."

"Ahh, this explains why I had had massive chest pain," I said, nodding. "I was not only picking up on *your* pain, but also on your daughter's pain!

I saw their spiritual daughter standing close to them. She was showing me something to do with a holiday.

"Are you planning on going on holidays somewhere soon?" I asked.

"No," Kym said, shaking her head. "Why?"

"Because she just said you have to go on a holiday."

"Huh, I wish," Kym said with obvious doubt.

"Your daughter says she wants you to go on a holiday, and I feel it will be around three months from now. I also feel it might be overseas, even if it's only to Tasmania – this is over the water and not very far away. I also see you going on a plane."

"I've been trying to get her to go on a holiday for a while," her husband piped up, "but if she is going on a plane, then I'm not going. I don't like planes!"

"Do you know anyone overseas?" I asked Kym.

"Yes," said her husband, brightening up, "her cousin lives in Tasmania!"

I could've fallen over.

"There you go," I added confidently. "You will be okay going on a holiday on your own!"

"Yes," Kym said, smiling.

I turned to her husband.

"How would you feel about being on your own for a couple of weeks?"

"I'll be fine!" he answered, smiling at Kym and putting his arm around her shoulders.

"It's important for you to go away for a while," I said to her earnestly. "It will make your daughter very happy. She can feel your sadness and pain and she knows how bad you feel about her passing. So you have to do this for your well-being."

Then I saw a spirit man with Kym and, not wanting to say anything to upset her, I looked for a way to say it.

"Do you know anything about computers? Because I can see you making something and selling it on-line, or through the internet."

"That's freaky!" she gasped. "Just before my Dad passed over – he passed about three years after our daughter went and he missed her terribly – he taught me everything I know about the computer!"

"I can see you going into a business with someone and this will help your finances pick up, so go for it."

"Oh my gosh!" Kym cried. "One of my daughters would like to have a business and I could help her with it!"

At this point I felt her shoulders were in some pain.

"Do you have any pain on your shoulders?" I asked.

"Yes."

I placed my hands on them, and gave a little massage, which seemed to help her. The daughter then asked for a special request, so I leaned in towards Kym's cheek.

"This is from your daughter," I softly said, giving her a little kiss. "She asked me to give you a hug, too and said not to worry, everything is going to be alright. And she is at peace, with no more pain, and is very happy."

I finished there and started to walk back to my stall.

"Don't worry, I'll be in touch!" Kym called, smiling. "Because I really would like to buy one of your books!"

I could also sense that she would want a reading then, too. I smiled and waved back and returned to my stall. About half an hour later, as things got quieter, my husband and I packed up and went home; I felt great for having helped this mother and daughter reconnect and also for not having any more chest pains!

At the next market a month later, Kym did return to see me at my stall and she bought my book as promised, which I signed for her, too. She also stayed for a reading.

೧೨

The Young Man and the Cemetery

On a dark and stormy night many years ago, I had the most unusual experience of my life…

I was driving home alone from a private reading some thirty kilometres away when I saw the car was low on fuel. Knowing there was a petrol station along the way, I headed for it. Under clear skies I pulled up to the bowser and filled the tank, noticing there was no one else around. It was late, and so not unusual for the place to be empty. I paid for the fuel and returned to my car, glad to be home soon.

I'd barely driven five minutes when rain suddenly started pouring down. Surprised, I reached to turn on the window wipers and thought I saw a movement in the rear-view mirror. My heart jumped into my throat – was someone there?

In awful silence I continued driving as lightning flashed and thunder rumbled around me. The storm seemed to have come from nowhere and looked to be set in for the night. A cold feeling ran through my body as I fretted about my situation. Was there an escaped criminal in the back seat? Were they going to harm me?

In the darkness inside the car and with the rain pelting down, I simply didn't know what to do. Should I speak to the person or ignore them? Could I hope it was only my imagination and that they would just go away?

As I passed under a lonely street light, I glanced in the mirror again – to see a young man's face, possibly in his late teens or early twenties.

He seemed agitated and looked a bit flustered. I decided to speak to him and gathered myself together, making my voice calm and controlled.

"Are you okay?" I asked.

But there was no answer. Just a blankness in return.

I waited a few more minutes, trying to observe what I could of him as I carefully drove on. There was still the fear that he might attack me in some way. I found myself mentally asking my guides for protection.

And then I thought, maybe he was simply wanting a lift to the town centre and had hopped in without asking because he was too shy to ask. Maybe he assumed I wouldn't mind him hitching a ride and would ask me to stop the car where he wanted to get out.

At around fifteen minutes from home I neared a T-junction in the road, where several street lights lit up the area and made it easier to see into the seat behind me. Through the mirror I saw how he watched this corner with increasing fear on his face, and there was a particular light pole that really bothered him.

I was scared in case he suddenly decided to jump out the door or worse, over into the front with me. But I worried unnecessarily, for nothing happened... yet.

I took the turn to the right and we continued in silence, though he kept staring back at the corner. It was almost as if he expected to see something there, or that perhaps he *was* seeing someone that I hadn't. Maybe it was a terrible memory for him.

I drove on rather anxiously, hoping he would settle down. The road passed a small, old cemetery that I didn't think was even in use any more and as we neared its entrance, he finally spoke up.

"Stop! Stop the car!" he called rather loudly.

I panicked and slammed on the brakes, thinking, '*Oh no, here it comes. My time's come and I'm going to die!*' It was a horrible feeling and I didn't know whether to start pleading for my life or scream for help.

But everything was quiet; there were no demands to get out, to hand over my purse or do anything else. Anxiously I looked in the mirror…

He wasn't there. Somehow he had gotten out without me hearing the door open or close. Suddenly, and with dread, I imagined him standing at my driver's door – just out of view – waiting to drag me from my car! Who knew what he'd do next? Though I shook with fear, I turned to face him, waiting for the worst.

But he wasn't standing beside my door. He wasn't about to threaten me.

He was across the road, walking through the cemetery gates, head down, hands in his pockets, without even a glance over his shoulder.

I didn't think any more about it. I put my foot on the accelerator as hard as I could in case he was going to return with some mates. I floored it the rest of the way home, not even considering if police were about. Strangely though, just a few minutes after leaving the area, the rain, lightning and thunder stopped as quickly as it had started.

But it was great to see my familiar driveway and also my understanding husband. Still reeling from my ordeal, I couldn't get in the house quick enough to tell him what had just happened.

"Would you make me a cup of tea please?" I begged him, shaking uncontrollably.

"Are you okay?" he asked. "You look like you've seen a ghost!"

"I hope not," I said, and explained to him what I had experienced.

He looked at me with a weird expression.

"Are you sure you don't know what happened in that area three months ago? Because it sounds like you really have seen a ghost!"

I was sure I didn't.

"No," I replied, trying hard to calm down.

"There was a young man who was just celebrating his eighteenth birthday," he began, "and had ducked out to that same garage station that you had stopped at to get some extra ice, drinks and food for his friends that were due to arrive at his place that night. He only lived a couple of kilometres away from it."

I almost fell off my chair.

"It happened three months ago today," Clive added. "It was raining when he hit a greasy patch on the road and fish-tailed all the way down to the corner, doing a ninety-degree turn at the T-junction. And he slammed into a telegraph pole there – right on the corner!"

I was shivering all over, remembering my drive through that section of road, where the lights lit up the inside of my car and I could see his terrified eyes.

"He was facing the opposite way when they found him," Clive went on. "His door was all crushed in. They said he would have died instantly."

My mind was awash with mixed feelings and images.

"He was nearly home," Clive said a little sadly. "The family buried him in the local cemetery there the following week."

"How do you know all of this?" I asked him.

"It was in the paper. Didn't you see it?"

"No," I replied, still dazed by the experience. "I don't read the newspapers. I don't have time to."

So now it all made sense; the frightened look on his face; the long stares at the light pole; his need to stop at the cemetery. He was going back to his 'new' home.

I suppose you could say that he did want a lift after all, and I was there to help him. But I let fear stand in the way and because he looked real rather than a spirit, I didn't stay to help him cross over into the spirit world. If ever it were to happen again I'll know what to do – help him walk through to the Light.

৺ଓ

Animals

Two Best Mates

There was another time when I was in the hall of my local spiritualist church, attending as host speaker for our two guest mediums that evening. I was sitting to the side of the platform next to them as they read for the audience. Opposite me, in the aisle of the fourth row, was a man whom I'll call Joe.

Whilst the mediums were busy talking, I saw the spirits of a beautiful Shepherd and a small dog, similar to that of a Jack Russell, appear. They walked in front of me and straight to Joe. The large dog tried to jump on his knees, but he couldn't do this too well, so he ended up just sitting beside his right leg. The Jack Russell managed to jump up onto his knee and happily curled up in his lap as though he needed a cuddle. I could feel the man's pain of having lost them, too.

When the service broke up for refreshments, I politely approached him, keen to talk to him about these two dogs.

"Hello," I said. "Did you used to have a Shepherd and a little dog like a Jack Russell?"

"Yes, I did indeed!" he replied, looking quite surprised. "Why do you ask?"

"It's just that while the service was on, I saw them walk in front of me and go right up to you."

"Really?" he said, with a bit of a laugh.

"Yes. The little one was sitting on your knee and the Shepherd was sitting to your right just there by your foot," I explained, indicating the spot where he'd settled.

The man looked there automatically, smiling, and a little sad.

"I watched the Shepherd try to climb up your legs, as though he wanted to get up to you, but he couldn't." I went on. "And the little dog wanted up, too. So he jumped up and curled on your lap. He looked very much like he wanted a cuddle."

"They were my boys," he said, his smile getting bigger. "I miss them very much, and I think of them quite regularly."

"I thought so. They seem very loyal to you."

"They were mates, these two," he agreed. "The Shepherd, Buddy, had arthritis in him, poor boy. He found it hard to walk towards the end. He passed over about five or six months before the other one. And the little one, Max," he added, "went downhill over the next few months after that. I think he missed his mate dreadfully. About six months later, he stopped eating and passed away one night in his sleep. I found him very cold the next morning in his little bed."

It was so sad to hear this, but I could see this man had needed to know these special friends of his were still there.

Grinning, he added, "Max appeared to have a smile on his face when he died, as though he had just found his long-lost friend!"

I agreed, giving him a nod.

"Well, they are both together again and are both very happy and well," I assured.

Joe had a tear in his eye.

"They're just letting you know that they're still with you. They are around you constantly."

This picked him up immensely.

"Thank you, Love. I needed to hear that," he said, smiling at me. "It's good to know they're not in any more pain and are together."

As we parted I thanked my angels for their guidance in showing me this man's pain: he could move on without worrying if his animals had ever found each other.

ಬಂಗ

The Lady Who had been a Horse

I remember one particular animal who came to me just as I was about to go to bed for the night. She first showed me her animal form – a beautiful brown, chestnut coloured horse with a fabulous blonde mane. Then she appeared to me as a tall blonde lady.

"Hello, I used to live on a farm," she began, sounding nice. "I was a racehorse in that life. I gave birth to three beautiful foals while I was there. Two of them went on to be champions," she continued, smiling. "I am so proud of them."

She described to me about her life on this farm, which she'd loved, and she also told me of her tragic death.

"The farmer gave me a hay bale to eat and went on with his chores. Just before grazing on it, I sensed danger nearby. Before I could turn around I felt a tremendous pain run up my leg. I tried to walk to the farmer not far away from me when I collapsed and fell into a deep sleep. It wasn't until later I realised that I had died and saw my body on the ground, and a black and red snake slithering away into the fields."

I felt so sad for her, hearing of the awful circumstances of her passing. It must have been very painful. But the lovely lady had more to say.

"The farmer saw it too and picked up his rifle and shot it, but it was too late for me," she added, looking a little sad. Then she brightened up. "But if you can please get a message to the farmer for me, and tell him that I'm fine and very happy, and I'm not in any pain! I have also met some beautiful spirits while over here with similar stories. I would be very grateful."

I looked at her earnestly and said, "Don't worry. I will find him and tell him for you."

She showed me images of the farm and its location, and also the farmer's face so I'd know where to go and who to look for.

I did eventually meet him and he was very happy to hear her story. He knew exactly which horse I was talking about, and the three foals she'd given birth to, too. I'm not sure if he really believed in any afterlife back then, because he was a little bit sceptical, but he did seem convinced that I'd had his mare come to visit me in the night.

When I told him that she was happy and had no more pain, he smiled, grateful for the news.

"Yes, she was a champion racer, though here she was in retirement," he said. "Lady Deanna; she was my favourite mare."

It was wonderful to be able to share this information with him, and even better that I was able to help this mare-spirit-lady make contact with her former owner.

୫୦୦ଓ

The Spirit Stag

I've seen many animal spirits in my life, most of them domestic, but also the occasional wild one comes to me from time to time. For instance, there was one day when Christine was sitting at our dining table in our Central Coast home and she asked if I could see anyone with her. When I looked at her, I saw a magnificent stag, standing just up behind her shoulder, as though he was watching over her. At this point in her life, Christine didn't understand how spiritual visions work, and what I described had puzzled her.

"What? How can he be standing *up* there when the floor is here?" she asked, referring to the height of the stag to the literal floor of the house.

"Well, he's in the forest, sort of on a mountain slope," I tried to explain.

"But how can there be a forest behind me when-" and she tapped the wall right beside her, "there's this wall there? We're in a house!"

"It's a vision," I said. "It may even be symbolic, although I feel that he is very real, too. It might be that he's your Spirit Animal."

She seemed to think on this, half smiling as she did. Christine has always loved these animals ever since she was a toddler, when she saw the movie *Bambi*, so I imagine that the idea of a wild stag appearing beside her meant quite a lot.

"That would be nice!" she said. "And it would make sense, knowing how much I love deer!"

"Yes, well, he's standing there looking very proud and protective-like," I went on, feeling better that she was happier. "He's got really big, beautiful antlers, and it's like he's watching over you lovingly, ready to fight anyone who might want to attack you."

Her smile got bigger.

"Hmm, I wish I could see him," she said wistfully.

"You can. You just have to close your eyes and clear your mind and let his image come into it!"

"Yeah but I want to be able to see him with my own eyes! Like you can!" she insisted. "You're actually seeing him with your real eyes now, aren't you?"

"Yes," I nodded, "but I'm also seeing a lot more with my Third Eye." I pointed to the middle of my forehead. "In there, that's where your Third Eye is. You learn to see the spiritual world with that. If you allow yourself to open up to it – and that's where you ask your Spirit Guides to help you – you will eventually be able to see spirits too!"

"Hmph," she grumbled, "I've tried that."

"I'm afraid that's a Gift that will have to come to you in time. If you're meant to have it, you'll have it."

"That's what I'm worried about," she said, downcast. "What if I never get that Gift?"

I looked at her a bit frustrated and said, "You can always ask for it."

"How?"

"You quietly meditate and ask your Spirit Guides to help you. They know what is best for you and they know if you're meant to have this sort of Gift or not. With practice and persistence, you may well be given this ability one day."

I don't think she was too convinced, going by her expression.

"You can also visualise a curtain in front of your mind," I added, to encourage her. "Pretend you're in front of a stage and its curtains are closed. When you're ready, try to open them with your mind and as they open, you wait to see people behind it, standing on the stage, ready to talk to you."

She was listening and nodding thoughtfully.

"For instance, you might see family members behind there, like Grandma or Grandpa. Or you might see friends you used to know from years ago. There might be a lot of people – the stage could be crowded with them, or you might only see a couple, and they might be your Spirit Guides or Guardian Angels, or just friendly spirits who want to talk to you. There's no right or wrong in who's there."

Well, it took her a number of years, apparently, because she's seen quite a few spirits since then, more so since she's been living with us and has given a lot more attention to this part of her life. Because she accepts there's an afterlife, and because she knows I've picked up on many things for people, she knows that when we die here, we only leave our physical bodies, and that we continue to exist in the spiritual dimension, watching over our loved ones who are still here.

ଽଠଓ

"Spirit Stag"
(Red Deer)

Sasha's Visit

Sasha was Christine's little dog, a white Maltese-cross. Her mother, Muffin, (who features on the cover of my first book), was a gorgeous brown Maltese-cross with, we think, silky terrier; she was our little angel. Sasha's father, Rusty, was also a cross-breed Pomeranian, though he did seem to have a Chihuahua look about him, too. The three of them were Christine's 'kids' and each one, in time, have passed on with age.

When first writing this part of this book, Sasha had only been gone a few months. She was very close to her "Mummy" and when Christine was studying at college, Sasha was left with Clive and I. Unfortunately, Sasha didn't much care for anyone else's company, as she was quite skittish and would more often than not spend the days tucked up on Christine's bed, waiting for her return. If I went near her, she would often cowl down or even run away, but on one particular day, she started to whine and wouldn't settle.

It was nearing midday and from the sounds she was making, I thought she must have been in pain. I went to the room, fully expecting her to shy away from me.

But to my surprise, she allowed me to pick her up – a rare thing indeed – and let me carry her outside, where I gently set her on the grass. She did her business and then again, allowed me to carefully scoop her into my arms. Promptly I put her back on my daughter's bed, in case Sasha needed Christine's smell to feel calm. But this wasn't to be.

By this point she was not only whining and whimpering, she also gave a little yelp. Then she broke into a howl, which she hardly ever did. It almost sounded as if she was literally saying, "Marm- I want my Marrmmy!"

It was painful to hear her crying so loud. I was so upset that I started to cry with her.

"Sorry Sasha," I said, while my eyes filled with tears, "I don't know what to do for you."

The mournful cries didn't stop, she was clearly distressed, and so was I. In desperation I rang the vet and, while talking to the receptionist, I couldn't stop crying while I tried to explain the little one's condition. The young lady on the other end heard Sasha's cries, too.

"Bring her straight down and we'll ask one of the vets to see her a.s.a.p.," she said.

I was so relieved. As I got her organised for the trip, I rang Christine to let her know what I was doing. All the while, Sasha was crying in the background and my tears were hard to keep under control.

"Okay, that's fine," said Christine. "You did the right thing. Get her down there as quick as you can. I'm packing my gear as we speak, so I'll meet you there!"

My daughter was there about five minutes before I arrived and quickly took her baby in her arms. The crying went on and it was dreadful to hear, for there didn't seem to be anything we could do to ease her pain. At least now, however, we were definitely in the right place. Christine held her as we waited for an available vet and when at last she could be seen to, the diagnosis wasn't good.

"It looks as if she may have suffered a stroke," the vet, Rob, said. "There's not a lot we can do for her, at least not without further tests or even x-rays. But she does show symptoms of this being the case. About all I can do at the moment is give her a needle to ease the pain."

Christine agreed and continued to hold her girl as the needle was given. But it was clear that after a few minutes, it had had no effect on her. All Sasha wanted to do was to cuddle into her mother's arms and cry.

"I'm not sure if tests will do any good," Christine said, her eyes full of tears. "She's fifteen, so she's old. It could be anything going on in there."

Although I hated the thought, I said, "Maybe it's time for her to go to 'doggy heaven'?"

Christine couldn't answer, but she sort of nodded.

"If you want, I could take her out to the other room and ask our senior vet for his input?" Rob offered.

Christine nodded and waited as he took Sasha to a room in the back of their practice for the senior vet to look at. When he returned, it wasn't any better.

"He seems to think she mightn't recover even if we do try something. We could operate on her to try fixing the situation, but even then, she still might not come through. It's your decision."

Christine took a deep breath, cuddling her baby on the examination table. "I think we should… let her go," she said, struggling with tears. "Maybe it's her time and at least she won't be in any pain then."

Rob watched on, not wanting to persuade her either way: it has to be the owner's decision.

"We'd better give her the needle," Christine finally said.

"Is this what you want to do?" Rob asked after a moment; he wanted to make sure it was *her* decision, not because of anything he might have said to influence her.

"Yes, I think it's probably for the best. I hate it, I really don't want to lose her, but it's most likely the best thing we could do for her."

Both Christine's face and mine were awash with tears as the vet prepared the needle. It's the hardest thing to see your babies go to sleep, knowing they will not reawaken and look into your eyes with love again.

Peacefully Sasha was sent on her way. It was a very sad home for a while after.

We cried for hours that night and I could see Christine wasn't taking her baby's passing very well. When I went to bed, I couldn't help thinking of Sasha. But when I woke up the next morning, I felt a presence around me – a tallish but slim lady, who I strongly felt was Sasha.

"Hello? Who are you? And what do you want?" I asked.

"I'm Sasha," she said, "and I want to give Mummy a message."

So she *was* Sasha in human form, which put me at ease then and I listened to what she had to say.

"Thank you for taking me to the Doggy Doctor," she said, "for I was in a lot of pain." (Doggy Doctor is Clive and I's nick-name for the vets that we often used when telling our little ones of their upcoming visits). She added, "Tell Mum I said thank you for giving me the needle, because I am not in any more pain."

She then said something that surprised me...

"Tell her that when you (meaning me), put me outside to do a wee, I felt a 'pop' go off in my tummy. This made my pain worse, but it only hurt for a little while. Now I am with angels and other animals like me, and my tummy doesn't hurt anymore. So please let Mummy know that I am not angry at her for doing what had to be done, for I couldn't bare anymore of the pain that I had, and it was not her fault. I'm grateful for the chance that I had with her and she was a great Mum to me and my family. I am with Muffin and Rusty and very happy."

I relayed all of this to Christine later that day. She was very teary, of course, but took heart that her 'daughter' was alright.

"You know," said Christine, trying to smile, "that's exactly how she would talk, if she were human. Those are the words she'd use, like "Mummy" and "wees"; because you say "piddle" for the number-ones, but I have always said "wees", or "wee-wees" to them.

"Well, I just want to let you know what happened to me this morning. I had to let you know that she'd come to me to tell you she's ok and that she's really grateful for what we did – and that she says you were a good mum to her and the others."

"Thank you, Mum," she said, wiping away the tears. "Yeah, I did need to hear that and although it doesn't take away the pain, it does make a difference to know these things. It means a lot." She sort of looked 'up'. "And thank you my baby girl," she said, crying but smiling. "Thank you for coming to Nanna and telling her all of that. You know I've been struggling with losing you and that I've probably been too emotionally hurt to pick up on you. I'm so glad you did talk to Nanna. Please know how much I love you."

༄༅

Thank you, Sasha, for coming to me that morning, for it made such a difference to us both to know we did the right thing, and that all is well with you and the others.

We love you still.

༄༅

Sasha

The Scared Collie Dog

One day, around four in the morning, I had a visit from my late Mum, Hilda.

"Do you remember the time when Tess was scared out of her wits?" she asked. Tess was Mum's tricoloured collie dog when I was young, who had lived with her in Dundas, N.S.W.

"About a week after Dad passed away; it was the day of Dad's funeral?" she said, "and I was walking towards the kitchen to lock up for the night."

"Yes, I do remember that night," I said to her in my mind. "I was sitting on the lounge when it happened."

"Tess slowly made her way down the hallway to my bedroom," she added.

"She loved to sleep on your bed with you two."

"I knew where she was headed and didn't think anything of it," Mum went on. "I was about to go down the hall shortly after her, but as I made my way towards it, I almost got bowled over!"

"Oh do I remember seeing how she'd come flying back down to the lounge with her tail between her legs!" I replied. "She was shaking so badly, as though she had seen a ghost!

Mum had called to her at the time, trying to coach Tess back, but she just wouldn't go near the hallway, much less the bedroom.

Mum and I had looked at each other, quite confused.

"Tess won't go down to the bedroom," she'd said back then. "I think she just saw Dad!"

We had wondered about it for days and no matter what we said or did for her, Tess simply wanted nothing more to do with the place. She had curled up at the side of the lounge near the front door, as far away from the hall as she could get.

"You could see she was scared out of her wits," Mum added, sharing the memory with me.

It was starting to make sense to me now, for Tess seemed to have changed since that night.

"And even after she'd died about three years later, she never went down near your room ever again!"

"Yes," said Mum, "she was never the same again."

ಬಂಛ

Mum, Hilda, and Tess, out in the front yard of their Dundas home.

Kitten by the Curtain

Some animal stories can be quite simple, like this one. I was called to a lady's house for a reading. We sat at the dining table next to a wall, when almost immediately, a small, spirit-kitten walked across it and curled up on the window sill across from us.

"Have you lost a small kitten?" I asked her. "It looks like a tortoise-shell, olive-green in colour, with black stripes down its sides."

"Yes!" she exclaimed. "She died of a tick bite only a month ago. She was only six months old, but she was adorable and I miss her terribly! How did you know?"

"She just walked across the table and curled up on the window sill over there," I said, pointing to it.

She gasped in shock.

"That's where she always slept most days! She loved that spot!"

When I finished her reading, she asked if the kitten was still there.

"No. She is happy though, and will often come back to that area from time to time. Just listen very carefully when it is quiet and you might hear her purring."

She seemed to relax then, probably to learn that her precious kitten is still around. I could feel the sadness disappear from her and knew she'd be fine.

༄༅

Dreams & Visions...

"The Dogs Are Okay"

It was nearing the fifteenth anniversary of my son's death in September 2012 when I had a strange dream of Arthur, which I believe was yet another encounter with him, and his way of saying "Hi" to me. The night before having this dream, I remember I had been thinking about him, and if he'd met up with the dogs we'd had when our kids were young. These were four Collie dogs, called Shelties, and all had since grown old and died many years ago.

We had gotten the male, "Sooty", as a pup when the kids were quite young. He was almost black all over, with a little bit of brown on his paws and face, and a lot of white on his chest and neck area. We bought "Cindy" about six months later, as company for him. She was a lovely sandy colour with a little white on her chest and neck.

Within a few years these two had had a litter of four pups, which we sold, but a couple of years later, they had a second litter of two pups – a boy, "Sandy", and a girl, "Kelly" – which we decided to keep. They both had their mother's colouring, though darker in shade. Arthur quickly took to Sandy, (whom he named himself), and my eldest daughter, Debbie, took in Kelly.

The kids loved growing up with these dogs, with Arthur and Sandy being quite close. Naturally, they went with us when we moved to W.A. and came back with us when we moved to the Central Coast of NSW, in September 1987.

We'd celebrated our first Christmas there when, on Australia Day 1988, Sooty died at the ripe age of eighteen. In September two years later, Cindy died. Both were sadly missed. Four years after Cindy's passing, Sandy began coughing up blood. He was found to have had a massive tumour in his chest and his condition was terminal. We had to put him to sleep as there was nothing we could do to ease his situation.

Arthur was devastated, for he worshipped his little boy, though he understood that both these 'pups' were now quite old themselves. Kelly had been experiencing a terrible skin disease for many months, which kept her constantly itchy, hot and greasy. We felt so sorry for her that within a couple of hours of Sandy's passing, we decided to end her suffering, too. Now the furry family would be all together.

So in this dream, I was back in the house where we'd lived, in our old hometown of the Hills District of New South Wales. The house itself was not exactly the same as the real one, but the backyard, back door and porch were very similar. I felt a bit strange, not really knowing why I was there.

Standing at the kitchen window, which looked out onto back yard, I could hear laughter and dogs barking outside. Drawn to the sounds, I walked to the back door and was amazed to see Arthur and the four Shelties on the lawn, playing tug of war with a piece of rope, or something like rope.

They all looked perfectly healthy!

Arthur looked up briefly and gave me a wave with his right hand, smiling brilliantly at me! It was wonderful to see. It was very much as though he knew I'd been thinking of them all and that I needed reassuring.

It felt like he was saying, "See? The dogs are okay. We all are!"

I felt honoured to know that he did this for me, and that the dogs *are* very happy and well in the spirit world. I woke up happy, feeling truly rewarded – I now know that I don't have to worry about them, or him, anymore.

ಬಡಚ

Sandy

The 'Boarding' House

While visiting Kevin in W.A. one time, I woke out of a weird dream which left me frustrated and bewildered, for I didn't know whether it had really happened or not. All I know is that in it, my best friend and I decided to go on a holiday somewhere and, with our bags packed, we headed off.

We arrived at the doorstep of what I'd call a dingy-looking, very old boarding home, though this didn't seem to worry us. We let ourselves in and walked down this dark hallway towards a large room. There we saw quite a few people. It was just like walking into a very large, old-fashioned foyer, or ornate lounge room. Even though it was well lit, it was rather dull looking.

I saw a man to my left, who appeared to be sitting in a wheelchair. He seemed grumpy, as though he'd had a bad day, or wanted to get out of this environment, for he was impatient and seemed ready to 'explode'.

The other people just stood around, chatting away, having a cup of tea or drinking something else. It was a bit like a quiet party; no one seemed to care that we had arrived, nor took any notice of us – we just blended in.

So we stood and watched, quietly observing everyone.

Through a large door of this room, in the far opposite corner to our left, there was another well-lit hallway and every now and then, someone was called to a room through there. They would go in, but never come back. So when this door opened on one occasion, we followed a person to see what was going on in there.

He went to the room and closed the door behind him. We waited there, a little unsure what to do next. Then all of a sudden it flung open and a large hand, visible up to the elbow, beckoned my friend in. She was sucked in, stomach first. Her body became shaped like a backward banana, with a trail of wispy-looking air spreading from her head and feet. It was very eerie to watch.

"Nooo!" I screamed. "Come back! You can't have her!"

Then a man's ordinary, clean-shaven, smiling face appeared.

He said nothing, but beyond him I could see several people in there, my friend among them. Then they were being lifted up, floating to the sky above. It looked like some sort of alien abduction at work. I was horrified! Suddenly I woke up, feeling that I was somehow spared.

Thinking over the dream, I feel it was showing me a way to heaven, or to some afterlife, and as it was not my time to go, I wasn't included in the ascension. But it's as if I have had to 'see' this example to know not to be scared when I do pass on.

ᛈᛉ

Julie and the Jockey

Sometime in the early 1990's, the spirit of a young lady, named Julie, came to me with a very disturbing message. Through visions, she told me a sad story of her life with her father, and how she had died because of the man she'd loved. I know that it's important for Julie to have her story included here, for she reminded me of it when I was writing my first book and the feeling that it must be shared has been very strong ever since. Perhaps you will see why…

Apparently, her father had owned a horse stud on which he'd trained racing horses. When she was in her early teens, Julie lost her Mum. In her late teens she fell in love with her father's jockey, whom we'll call Danny. Only thing was, her father objected to the 'happy romance' side of Julie's life. He liked Danny as his jockey, but he didn't fancy him as a son-in-law.

The father was a plump, robust man who had big ideas for her to meet – and possibly marry – the son of one of his rich friends. His attitude was that it was one thing for her to be friendly with the jockey, but romance was out! So she had to meet Danny in secret.

Danny lived on the property in a little cottage behind the stables, and it was here the couple would privately spend their time together.

Julie's father regularly hosted large parties, where he'd entertain his rich friends and associates. He'd have these parties organised every one to two months apart, so that his daughter would eventually meet the 'right man for her'. But Julie didn't enjoy them, wanting instead to be with the man she felt was her true love; Danny. She took to sneaking off during these occasions and hiding away with him in his cottage.

When her father learned of her secret visits with Danny, he hired a private investigator to watch her.

At the next party, soon after her twentieth birthday, Julie pretended to be sick, saying that she wished to stay in her room. She waited until the party was well under way before sneaking down the stairs to the back door, and went to see Danny.

She didn't realise the private detective was watching her. He saw her go to the cottage and discreetly followed her.

By now Julie considered Danny as being her boyfriend. They talked of a future together and decided to marry on her twenty-first birthday. Then they decided to run away the next morning. The detective overheard their conversation from the window and soon left to tell her father.

The very next day, her father gave her some terrible news.

"I've arranged for you to visit your aunt," he'd said. This aunty lived some three hours away. "You'll stay with her for a few months so you can sort out what you will do for the future."

Naturally, Julie protested. "Why? I don't need to sort anything out. I know what I want to do!"

"No," came the determined reply, "I feel that you need a break from the farm life."

"But I love the farm! It's my world!" she cried.

"Yes, well it's already decided," her father firmly said.

"But what about Danny?" she insisted. "I'll miss him terribly!"

"You won't be seeing in him anymore. Go pack your bags. You're going today."

Her father hadn't revealed to her yet what he'd been told by the detective, and she was oblivious as to why he was making her leave so quickly, without any discussions. Though she was sent to her room, Julie defiantly slipped out the back door and went straight to see Danny to tell him about her father's mean decision.

She couldn't find him at his cottage and wondered where he could be.

She noticed blood on the carpet and, thinking he'd injured himself, thought he'd gone to the doctors. It hadn't occurred to her that foul play may have been behind it. She returned to the house, disappointed.

"Where's Danny?" she'd asked her father.

"Oh, I think he might have had a better offer, because I found a letter this morning, saying he had to go interstate to help his friend out."

Julie was puzzled; Danny had said nothing of it the night before.

"Why didn't you tell me about it a minute ago?" she demanded.

"I didn't mention it to you because I didn't think you would be worried, seeing as how you were only *friendly* with him," he commented in an off-handed way. "It's not as though you were in love with him, because I know it wasn't serious."

According to Julie's spirit, it was around this time she smelled a rat. There was nothing to say except to ask if she could see the letter.

"I thought there was no point in keeping it so I threw it in the fire out of disgust," he quickly responded. "I was angry with him for leaving us like that after all I've done for him!"

Julie knew there was more to this story than he was admitting.

"I'll go to my Aunt tomorrow, if that's what you really want for me," she said.

That night, she went to visit her two friends, who also lived on the same property about fifty metres away, directly across from the stables and directly behind her very large home. These two, a man and his wife, ran the tea and coffee-come-wine bar shop for the staff, and visitors who would stay over. They were very good friends with her father and thought they may have known what happened to Danny.

They served her wine to relax her, and after drinking some of it, she asked them if they knew where he was.

"We thought we heard noises coming from his room," they said.

"What time would this have been?" she asked, not telling them that she had left his company around ten-thirty that night.

"It was possibly around eleven-thirty when we thought we heard a struggle," the husband began. "But we didn't want to investigate in case he had had a lady friend over and was just having a romping session."

"We thought we'd just leave well enough alone," the wife added. "We didn't want to interfere with his personal life."

By now Julie was starting to feel drowsy, thinking she must have had too much to drink.

"I'll just sit down on the lounge, if you don't mind," she said, going to the comfy seat.

In the images she showed me, as she turned to the lounge, she noticed a man outside throw something like a round ball towards the front door of her house, right under the window of her father's study. Confused, Julie sat down, then noticed the couple going out the front door and hearing it lock behind them.

She tried to say something to them, but then she heard a very loud bang and saw the front of her home explode. Julie blacked out at this point, not knowing what had happened.

When she opened her eyes, she saw her mother and boyfriend standing in front of her, with their arms outstretched, telling her to come with them to a better place.

"Is Dad okay?" she asked them.

"Do not worry, Julie," she was told. "He's gone to another place to sort out his problems."

It was now that she finally found out the truth.

"He was no good, Love," her mother went on. "When you were young and I got sick, he smothered me. He wanted my life insurance money to fund the farm."

Julie was shocked.

"He had your jockey friend murdered, after you left his room that night, by the investigator," her mother added.

"He slit my throat," Danny said, "because he didn't want us to get married."

"And you were poisoned by your friends because in the will, your father left the farm to their care if anything was to happen to you or him; they were to inherit only part of the farm for their years of dedication to him."

"Why them?" Julie asked, a little dazed.

"He liked their loyalty," was the simple answer given.

"I guess I was in their way then..." she murmured.

"He promised the investigator a couple of his prize racehorses as payment for killing me, too," said Danny, sadly. "So with no boyfriend to help you out, you were vulnerable."

"And with no man to share my inheritance, they stood to gain a lot," said Julie, understanding the situation for what it was.

"They had to get you out of the way and made it look like you were depressed and took your own life."

"So your father got what he deserved for being ruthless," her mother said, taking Julie's hand. "And now you can have a happy life here with us, helping others to overcome their grief."

৪০৪

After this visit from Julie, I happened to have been meeting a client for a reading at a coffee shop in town. She'd had a girlfriend with her, who had stayed behind when the session was finished. I don't remember how we came to be talking about Julie, this many years down the track, but what was revealed was so very uncanny.

I'll call her Dianne and back then, she was a medium in the learning phase, who was perhaps not strong enough to have received messages directly from Julie. I had told her of this story, which may have been prompted by the news of several scandals in the Australian horse racing industry of the day, such as possible horse doping to rig races. But Julie had also come to me during this conversation with Dianne, and her presence felt quite strong.

"My brother owned a stud farm out from Newcastle," Dianne had said, amazed and deeply shaken by what Julie had revealed. "He bred champion racehorses. But I'd had no idea that any of this had happened!"

"What do you mean?" I'd asked, not understanding.

"I know who you're talking about. That sounds like my niece," she'd said, quite seriously. "Julie was supposed to come stay with me at my house. I was expecting her, but she didn't turn up."

I couldn't believe what I'd just heard.

"I had wondered why she didn't arrive, back then," Dianne had continued. "It wasn't until later that week when I found out she'd died."

"Well," I'd said softly, "I'd like to think justice was done to those behind the murders. But if not, they will be judged when it's their time to go, for Spirit has a way of dealing with killers."

"I'm grateful for you telling me this story, Joyce," she'd said, smiling a little. "I didn't realise how severe it was. I thought it was just an accident!"

I hope that Julie, her Mum and Danny can rest in peace knowing that their story has finally been told. A big thank you to all of my beautiful spirit friends.

ෂ☯ෆ

Kissed by the Angel of Death

Another dream I'd had was of going for a short drive into the country to clear my head. I felt as if I needed a break from the noise and busyness of life. Unbeknown to me, this journey was about to show me something very interesting about the afterlife.

I had driven for about two-and-a-half hours when I felt the urge to slow down, to take in the beautiful scenery. Then everything seemed to be glowing – the trees seemed greener, the air smelt fresher, the sky looked bluer, even the sun appeared to be brighter. I couldn't have asked for a better day.

As I rounded a bend in the road I came across a sign, saying, "Rest Centre" and, "Lookout 500 metres ahead". So I slowed down and turned into the clearing, pulling up near the amenities block to freshen up. After I left the washroom I stood and observed the area while taking a deep breath, smelling the fresh, pure air. I couldn't believe I had never seen this place before. It was absolutely beautiful.

I had a light snack at a Kiosk a few metres away then ventured towards the lookout. Though a little rocky, it proved to be well worth the climb, for the view was breathtaking. I found it hard to tear myself away but alas, I realised I had spent too long there and needed to get back home.

I made my way down the rocky path to some roughly cut steps in the side of the mountain, where I tripped on a tree root that was sticking up over one of the steps. I must have hit my forehead before rolling onto my back, because I blacked out. I don't know how long I was out to it, but when I opened my eyes there was a man standing beside me, wearing a black suit. His hand was reaching out to me as though to help me get back up. He smiled warmly but didn't speak a word. He just waited for me to take his hand.

My instinct was to trust him, as I felt he knew what to do and where to take me for treatment. I knew I needed help of some kind because my head was hurting and I felt blood running down the side of my face. I could feel my body urging me to stand and to go with this stranger, when I noticed a brilliant white cloud appearing before us!

The man indicated for me to go with him into the cloud. I was overwhelmed, yet strangely felt at peace with his gesture, so I followed him. As we walked through the cloud I instinctively knew that I was going to be alright, for I didn't feel any danger around me.

On the other side of the cloud was quite a long sort of driveway, leading towards a very large white building with lots of windows. The man took me to the main doors where two men in white uniforms greeted us. He pointed at them, silently indicating for me to go with them. As I walked to the doors with these two other men, I looked back at him.

He was waving me on, still smiling and in my mind, I heard him say, '*Do not be afraid as they will make you better.*'

I gave him a big smile and followed the two men through the main doors into a foyer. It was unbelievably breathtaking in there! It looked like a huge hospital; the two men could've been male nurses for all I knew. I really felt like I was being watched over by angels, and I didn't care what happened to me, for I knew I was in good hands.

The men led me down the hall towards a lift. We went up two floors then walked to a second doorway on the right and into a large room, which had lights above an operating table. There were two lovely looking, angelic-like ladies there, and a man dressed in a white uniform, much like a doctor. They were all surrounded in a brilliant white, misty cloud and smiling at me.

The doctor gestured for me to get up on the table, which was high for me. But as I approached it, I felt the ladies lifting me up, almost as though I was floating in their arms! They laid me down on my back very gently and made me comfortable. It was unreal, for I had never experienced anything like this before.

They stood on each side of me, with the doctor behind my head, then all three of them raised their hands above it. Next, he lowered his hands to rest them just over my forehead. There were no tools or needles to be seen and though I wasn't frightened, I did wonder if anything would hurt.

He held them there for a few minutes then moved each hand to the opposite side of my brow, near to my ears. I waited for something to happen, like a buzzing sound or a perhaps an electrical vibration through my brain. Nothing. After what seemed like five minutes, I felt totally calm, relaxed and well. In fact, I felt warm all over.

Then, apparently, they were done: there was even a dressing put on me! The angel-ladies moved back to stand on one side of the bed, and the doctor looked down at me with a smile. He indicated for me to sit up, which I did, then he gestured for me to stand up. As before, I was amazed with the feeling of floating in the ladies' arms.

'*That was quick,*' I kept thinking. '*No pain killers, no cutting my head open, no dressings – no nothing!*'

They indicated for me to go back to the two waiting men. It was all so strange as no words were ever spoken, yet I seemed to understand them perfectly. As I walked out of the operating room I looked back at the table where I had lain – the room was empty! I was frustrated because I wanted to say "goodbye" and "thank you" to them for healing me. But something told me that they already understood.

The two men in white walked me back out to the main front doors, pointing to the very first man in the black suit, who waited for me in the long driveway. This first man, on seeing me, held out his hands and led me back to the white cloud. I just knew everything was going to be fine, though I was still curious about my strange situation.

I think we were in the cloud – or the driveway – when I whispered my thoughts to him.

"Where am I?" I asked. "What has just happened to me?"

He simply smiled at me, leaned forward and kissed me gently on my forehead.

"It's not your time yet," he whispered back.

Grateful for his help, I returned the kiss on his cheek, saying, "Thank you."

Instantly I woke up on the ground where I had fallen. I was being cradled by a pretty lady, and a man next to her was frantically talking. I don't remember too much about them, but they were both young and wearing bicycle gear.

"Are you okay?" he kept asking.

I tried to nod but the lady soothed me.

"Just lay still," she whispered close to my ear. "The ambulance will be here shortly. We thought we had lost you, but you will be alright now."

"What happened to me?" I asked, anxious to know.

"You just had a little accident," she gently said, "but everything is fine now."

In the background I heard the familiar sound of an ambulance's siren.

In moments, it seemed, two men in white uniforms came up to me, quickly setting up their emergency equipment. They checked me over for any fractures and cleaned my bleeding forehead.

"You're a lucky lady that someone saw you fall and called us straight away," they said. "And that we were able to find you so quickly."

I looked at the lady who had been cradling me; she waited to one side with a warm smile.

"How long have you been with me?" I asked her.

But the paramedics answered instead, as though she wasn't even there. I thought this was very rude of them.

"Oh only a few minutes. Someone rang about ten minutes ago for help and here we are." They quickly changed the subject by asking me the usual questions, like what's my name, where was I from, what's my date of birth and things.

"Do you know what's happened to you?" they asked me.

No! I didn't! It's what I had been trying to ask everyone else!

"I had been walking down the path," I began, feeling a bit groggy. "I remember going down some steps."

The nice lady silently indicated the tree root with her gaze – which I could sort of see now behind one of the paramedics.

"I… caught my shoe, I think…"

"How long do you think you've been here for?" he checked.

"Possibly ten to fifteen minutes, tops," I said. Surely it couldn't have been very long.

"Do you know what time this happened?" he asked.

I shrugged, trying to recall how my afternoon had played out. There was the drive, the stop at the kiosk, the walk up to the lookout and the long time I stayed there, then the walk back. I remembered seeing "Two-thirty" on my watch before leaving the lookout; it was that which had made me realise I still had a couple of hours to get back home.

"I think it was around two-thirty, why?"

"Are you sure?" he checked, sounding doubtful.

"Yes. I had just finished my lunch and decided to go for the walk up the mountain. I stayed up there for about an hour at the lookout." In the meantime, I kept wondering why he wasn't asking the lady, who just stayed quietly in the background. "Why are you so concerned?"

The man looked at his workmate. "Well, you are extremely lucky, as it is now three-thirty," he said. They'd finished tending to me and were in the midst of packing up. "We only got the call ten minutes ago. We were here practically straight away. So you must have been out for at least an hour." He glanced at me. "Someone must have been watching over you. Just as well we found you soon enough." He turned away, adding with a bit of a laugh, "It wasn't your time to go."

A chill ran through me. I'd only just heard those words said by that man in black! *'Had I just been in a dream, or did it really happen?'* I thought.

When they were satisfied that I appeared to be well enough, they asked if my head felt funny at all. They wanted to make sure that I wasn't the least bit giddy or feeling as though I was going to faint. Just then a call for an ambulance came over their walkie-talkies. A car accident had occurred further up the road, just north from here and it sounded pretty bad. Apparently this unit was the closest one to it.

"We're gonna have to go to that," the second paramedic said to his mate, who nodded.

"If you feel safe enough to drive, we want you to go steadily," he said, looking at me firmly. "Take it easy and don't rush. If you start to feel giddy or faint, pull over. Either go straight home or to the nearest hospital." It seemed a bit of a blur from there; they helped me back to my car then hurried to their ambulance and took off at a roaring speed, siren blowing, going in the opposite direction to me.

I tried to collect myself before starting the engine when I suddenly remembered the youngish couple who had sat with me on the path. I looked for them, wanting to wave to them and thank them for being there to help me. Only, I couldn't see either of them.

'That was odd,' I thought to myself. *'They soon disappeared. They must have been in a hurry to go somewhere. Maybe I held them up from something important?'* I was upset that I didn't get to say goodbye to them, nor thank them properly. I drove off with mixed feelings, being very careful of my driving ability and keeping a direct route for home.

But the dream hadn't ended there...

I was still quite shaken about the whole thing on that drive south from the mountains and I couldn't stop feeling like someone was watching my every move. It was a weird sense of both 'good vibes' and 'bad vibes', but that the good ones overrode the bad ones. My dream-self continued to question if any of this was for real – surely the man in black, the massive cloud and all that other-worldly stuff was just imagination?

By the time I had gotten home I must've convinced myself that I had fallen asleep up at the lookout and that the entire experience was down to an over-active imagination!

As I approached my neighbourhood, I began to feel a lot calmer. It was as though my body had undergone a real makeover and it felt refreshed. I put the car into the garage with a huge sigh of relief, went in and made a cuppa and decided on a whim to put the T.V. on; it was News Hour, so I settled in to watch it.

Then came the shock. A reporter was standing on a winding highway, talking about a dreadful accident between a red sedan car and two cyclists. In a daze I watched the footage – police blocking the road in the background, a yellow car smashed in at the front, a crumpled bicycle near it and a second one off the roadside in the long grass. I remember hearing the reporter describe what had happened...

"There's been a horrific accident today. Just before three this afternoon, a young couple were cycling up this highway, when a yellow car, travelling south and driven by a man aged in his late thirties, hit the red sedan, who had been driving just ahead of the cyclists. They were also going up this hill."

The news footage showed two crumpled bicycles not far from a parked truck. As the reporter spoke, I was actually seeing it happen.

"It's believed that the yellow vehicle had overtaken this slow-moving removalist truck, just as the sedan and the two riders were coming north. The two cars hit head-on at high speed, causing the yellow vehicle to flip and roll, striking the truck on the side and causing some damage to the driver's cabin. The sedan careered backwards, straight into the cyclists, who were right behind them at the time. Paramedics at the scene say that they were killed instantly and that the occupants of both cars are seriously injured. The driver of the removalist's van is lucky to escape with minor cuts and bruises…"

"No joke," I murmured, shaken with fear.

But another surprise was in store.

The pictures of the cyclists appeared on the screen – the same two people who had been with me at the lookout! I could not believe it!

"But I've just been with them…" I said, unable to settle.

"…It's expected that charges will be laid against the driver of the Commodore…"

A string of thoughts were running through my head: is this why the pair had disappeared after the ambulance men had helped me? Had they already died and somehow found their way to me at the lookout not far from them? But if they weren't really there, then who rang for the ambulance?

I touched my forehead, wondering, worrying, and just a little bit scared that it had all really happened. I could feel the bruise on my temple and the sticky bandage that had been put there to stem the bleeding. That part of my head hurt… What on earth had happened to me?

When I actually woke up in bed from this dream, my forehead ached so deeply as if it had been hit quite hard. I took a long time to gather myself, honestly feeling as if I had been that person who had walked up to the lookout, who went into the heavenly hospital, had met the two cyclists and also the ambulance men. The detail was so, so incredible and the experiences too uncannily real.

Some people might say it was just a dream, but I am quite certain that, for at least the two cyclists, they *were* there on that highway and *had* been killed in the way described on the dream-news.

༄༅

A Family Reunion… of sorts

This is a dream I'll never forget for a *very* long time – if ever. I found myself standing on a cliff surrounded by white fluffy clouds. A rickety sort of wooden bridge went off into the clouds ahead of me, to another cliff several feet away, that could be just seen through the mist.

I remember thinking of Arthur and my Dad, wishing I could see them or even visit them for a while. All of a sudden, I felt drawn to walk onto this bridge. At first I was hesitant, but soon felt confident that all would be okay and as I got closer to the end of the bridge, I felt the presence of an old man around. Even though I couldn't see him, I knew it was safe to keep going.

Then a hand appeared, extending to me through the misty cloud. Sure enough, on the opposite cliff stood an old man in a long white gown, with a long white beard and long white hair. No words were spoken but I felt he was beckoning me, and telling me not to be afraid. Once I was standing beside him, he spoke with his mind.

"Whom do you seek to find?"

"I would like to see my late son, my mother and father, and relatives if I could," I replied, thinking this was all so unreal. "Can you help me?"

The man turned around and pointed behind him, saying, "Come this way."

We seemed to glide through the cloud for only a second or two, when this whole new world appeared.

There were trees, hills and lots of greenery, almost like looking down at a large, open park; it was beautiful!

"What are their names?" he asked when we'd stopped.

"Arthur and David Duncan," I said.

He opened a book – that he was now holding – almost the size of a very large bible. He looked over one page and then another.

"Oh, here we are," he said, and then he floored me.

"Have you come to stay with us, or are you just visiting?" he asked politely.

"Just visiting, if I may," I replied, feeling a little nervous. At least, I didn't *think* I had come to stay!

He made a note in his book, then pointed down to the parkland. "Do you see that large tree over there?"

"Yes, but which one? There are quite a few."

"That one, near the little bridge over the stream."

I saw a tiny, red-railed, Chinese-style arched bridge over a small brook, situated just near a magnificent willow tree. People were milling around beneath its long leaves, as if waiting for me. "Oh, the big Weeping Willow tree?" I checked.

"Yes. Go across the bridge to the tree and see your family there."

"Thank you," I said, looking forward to meeting them. But I was confused as to how to get there. "How do I get down?"

"Don't worry about it, just think about them and you'll be there. When your time's up, you will hear a soft bell. Then you must return here to me so I can see you safely back to your world and family."

"Thank you," I said, and turned to see the waiting people. Thinking of my son and family, I felt myself gliding down to the bridge. Next thing I had crossed over it, now seeing their warm, smiling faces. Arthur saw me and stood up, then my father and mother followed him.

"I'm sorry to have left you the way I did, Mum," Arthur said, giving me a big hug. "But I was lonely and very depressed."

"That's okay, pet," I said, holding him tightly. "I know. I miss you so much and I love you, too!"

He stood to my right so that my father could hug me.

"Thank you for helping me to understand how to communicate with you in the hospital," Dad said. "It was ingenious!"

"Oh that's alright! At least we could communicate! I miss you so much, Dad!" He moved to my left as Mum stepped forward.

"Thank you for helping me to cross over," she said, hugging me tightly. "We all had a ball. I love you for that."

"That's wonderful, Mum," I replied. "I'm glad you caught the bus. I love you too." When Mum was dying in hospital, I whispered in her ear to look out for the bus that was coming to pick her up. She obviously caught it, and got a ride to heaven.

Other family members were also there and one by one they rose and rushed to greet me. No words were actually spoken, as it was all conveyed through our thoughts. We knew what each other was saying without having to speak it. I felt honoured to be in their presence and overwhelmed with excitement. The atmosphere was a lot like being in a group of people at a club, with everyone talking together, laughing, enjoying each other's company.

I turned back to Arthur, to see my in-laws smiling, also pleased to see me. Clive's mother and father greeted me warmly, and three of their adult sons, who have also passed over, welcomed me too.

When it seemed that everyone had come to say hello, two more people stood waiting. My lovely niece, Tina had a big smile on her face and she cuddled me close.

"Thank you, Aunty Joyce, for hearing me and taking notice of me after I came over here," she said. "That made me happy you spoke for me at the beautiful funeral Michelle gave me. I know you were hurting, but it did make a difference, thank you."

Her father was there, too and right after their visit, she faded away. Then I realised that I, too, was drifting backwards from everyone. It was a gentle feeling of being slowly pulled away from that scene. That's when I heard the sound of soft bells ringing – it was time for me to go. As I left, I watched my family and friends waving goodbye and throwing kisses to me, with smiles on their beautiful faces.

Then I was back on top of this mountain, feeling excited and relieved to be standing next to the same, angelic old man. He took my hand.

"It's time for you to return home," he said.

We faced the rickety bridge and I floated across it to the other side.

When I woke up, I saw that it was four-thirty-three in the morning and I wondered... did this really happen?

I believe it did.

৩০৫৪

My Vision of Madeline

Editor's NOTE: The following chapter contains descriptive content of an actual person. It is important to recognise that, at the time of publication, the person described here is still believed to be missing. Neither the parents of this person, nor anyone associated with her, or him, endorse this content, nor its author. The entire content of this chapter is purely of the personal view of its author.

In early August 2013 I was woken up around two in the morning by this almighty vision of a very young girl, who had just been telling me a bizarre story. At first, confused and in a daze, I didn't know what to make of it, yet it was too real to forget – or ignore. It had started with her calling out to me...

"I'm alive! I'm alive!" she anxiously cried.
"Who are you?" I asked, tuning in.
"I'm Maddie, Maddie McCann!"

I couldn't believe what I had heard; this, apparently, was the little child who had gone missing in Portugal. Having to trust this voice, I listened closely, as it was obvious she needed to talk to someone about her situation. As she talked, the scenes began appearing of the people and places she described.

"I was kidnapped while I was asleep. I was woken up by a noise. I thought it was my Daddy coming in to check on me, so I half sat up to say "Hello" to him. But it was a strange man coming into my room. He put something smelly over my mouth and I went back to sleep. I felt him wrapping me up in a blanket and thought I must have died because I could see him carrying my body."

I 'saw' this man as being smallish and thin in build, and the vision showed me Madeline in his arms, just as though she herself was watching what happened from outside of her body.

"He went outside and crossed over the road," she went on, "and went down the road very quietly, and very close to where Mummy and Daddy was sitting at the table."

This looked to be a barbecue type of setting, where her parents sat with some other people.

"I tried to call to them but they couldn't hear me. The man went around the corner then crossed back over to the other side of the road to another house, not very far, just up the road from my Mummy and Daddy. He took me into it and put me down on to his couch."

Here the man met up with a woman and spoke to her in a foreign language.

"I lay very still because I couldn't move. He spoke to a lady in a funny way. I didn't understand what he said, but it sounded like she called him "Joe", or something like that."

It seemed about a half-hour passed when a man pulled up in a dark coloured car outside. He came in, and also spoke in a foreign language. He gave the first man a lot of money and then carried Madeline out to the car, where he put her on the back seat next to a thin-built lady. She was dressed in a dark coloured dress with a black or dark blue scarf over her head and mouth.

"She looks a bit like Mummy," Madeline said of this second woman. "He put my head on her knee."

I saw the woman gently stroking her head. Madeline looked to be asleep through it all, though she said she knew what was going on because, "it was like I was floating around in the car, and I was able to see them somehow".

Then the car drove off very fast.

"We drove for a long while in the dark," she said.

When the sun was just coming up the next morning, they went around a roundabout, now in a very different place.

"I could smell the sea and I could hear the waves hitting the rocks, and there were a lot of bird noises," she added.

They sounded like seagulls. The car went up to a crossroad, turned right and stopped at another house not far from the ocean. She could still hear waves hitting the rocks, and was put into another bed here, where she woke up a little while later.

"I think the lady wants to keep me," Madeline said, "but I want Mummy and Daddy!"

I found myself wondering whereabouts she was located. Madeline must have picked up on this, for she showed me a map of where she thought she may have been taken to. She pointed to Spain, then Portugal and back to Spain, but she seemed to be confused, as was I.

I can only think that she was bewildered as to why she was taken there at all, and also of why she had been taken from her family. She couldn't understand what they were saying, which made things harder, I guess, but she did hear the name George.

He was a thick-set man of average height, "a bit like my Daddy's height", as she'd put it, and he was the man who had paid the money to "Joe" and driven the car to the new location.

But I also wondered if 'George' could be the name of the town, or the street name she was taken to, as in "St.

George", or "Georgetown", or "George Street". Or he may have had a similar last name. Unfortunately, in my sleepiness and her distressed state, it was difficult to be certain how or where the name came into it exactly.

After she told me her story I jumped out of bed and hurried down the hallway to the lounge room to write it all down. I passed Christine on the way, who was just returning from the back door after having let our dogs outside.

"What's the matter?" she asked.

But I couldn't speak for fear of losing this fascinating information. I shook my hand her way, wanting to stop her from distracting my thoughts.

"Shh!" I urgently said. "She's alive! She's alive!"

"Who's alive?" she asked, very puzzled.

"Madeline is. Madeline McCann is!"

I grabbed a pen and notebook and tried to begin. Christine sat on the lounge across from me, watching what I was up to.

"If you can't sleep and you are going to stay up, I'll wait until you are finished writing and we could play a game?"

Both of us would often have difficulty sleeping through the night and sometimes, if it was bad enough, we'd plug in the computer to the TV and play away. But not this time. I was too engrossed in Madeline's story and couldn't answer her. I had to concentrate. After about ten minutes, she left me to go back to bed.

I don't know how long I wrote, but I ended up filling several pages and even drew a sketch showing the round corner where she was carried from the hotel to the first house. As it turned out, I got a shock a couple of weeks later when the very same corner was shown in a news article of Madeline!

When I did get back to bed in the early hours before dawn, my sleep had been restless, for I couldn't let it go.

After breakfast that morning, I told Clive and Christine of this strange encounter in more detail. I felt so compelled to do something about it that I pestered them to help me get in touch with the police in London.

"Will you be going on-line today? Because I can't access the internet on my computer and I want you to contact Scotland Yard and tell them of my vision."

"They probably won't believe you..." she said with a doubtful look, "You know what police are like."

"Yes, but some are okay. Sometimes you'll get one or two who are prepared to listen."

"Hmm, I know what you're saying, but I don't know," she said, shaking her head; she wasn't convinced we'd be successful. "They're likely to write you off as a crackpot! I mean, they don't know who you are. And they're bound to get loads of other people claiming to be psychics calling in with stuff."

"I still want to try," I said determinedly.

"Well, I don't mind. I can help you go on-line in a little while. Otherwise Dad might be going on sooner."

"Would it be better if I just sent them a letter by ordinary mail?" I asked.

"It's up to you. I'd be surprised if they even look at it – email *or* posted letter!"

We stalled that morning, wondering what to do when a short time later, we heard an update on the TV.

"We have breaking news that Scotland Yard has just revealed they have news that Madeline McCann is still alive," the announcer said. "More will be available on tonight's news."

I was shocked, for I had not sent anything through to them yet! Then I realised that someone had obviously given them a tip-off or something. I felt there was little I could do but hope that they find her soon. I went ahead and wrote them a long letter, explaining to them everything Madeline had shown me.

Sadly, I've not heard from Scotland Yard in the years that have followed, and my senses tell me that it may well be too late to ever retrieve her.

ಬೊಲ

At the end of October 2013, another unusual thing happened...

At around one-thirty in the morning, while again trying to sleep, I felt someone sit on my foot. At first I thought of was one of my puppies and so reached for the torch and pointed it at the side of the bed where I expected to see one of them. But to my surprise, no one was there!

I turned off the torch and lay back down. Then I felt a hand on my ankle, moving slowly up towards my knee.

I jumped, thinking it may have been Christine come to ask me something, so on went the torch to see her.

But again, no one was there.

'*That's strange...*' I thought, turning off the light.

And there he was.

The figure of a small boy was standing next to my feet.

He looked to be about eight or nine years of age, with dark, shoulder-length hair curled upwards to just below his ears. He also had a fringe which curled under, and the style of it, to me, was just like looking at an old-fashioned photograph.

'*Who are you?*' I mentally asked him.

He started to fade away.

Then a young girl came into view, who looked like an older version of Madeline McCann, also around the age of nine or maybe ten years.

'*Madeline, is that you?*' I asked.

She faded but the boy reappeared.

'Who are you?' I asked him again. '*And what is your name?*'

He answered with only one word.

"Carlos."

Then he faded away, and the young girl returned.

'*Who are you?*' I tried yet again. '*Are you Madeline?*'

She looked quite seriously at me and also gave only one name.

"Carlotta."

She faded away, too, and this time neither child came back.

I was confused and tried to analyse what they may have been trying to say to me. All I could think of was that if this *was* Madeline McCann, was she trying to say something about her present circumstances?

Perhaps I had sensed her trying to tell me that she had been given to a couple, who wanted a little girl as a companion for the son, who was called Carlos.

Or was it that the couple she was with were named Carlos and Carlotta? Or maybe they were brainwashing her into thinking her real name was now Carlotta, and that they had changed her image to look like a boy so people wouldn't recognise her as the missing girl, Madeline?

I couldn't work it out, for there wasn't enough information to be sure about her situation. I spent some two hours thinking about it when sleep eventually caught up to me. But I was restless and woke up at eight o'clock that same morning, distraught and feeling like I had been dragged through a whirlpool backwards.

In the months and years since then, I have often thought of that night, and of the visions Madeline had shown me of being abducted.

It feels to me that she *had* been brainwashed into thinking she is the child of the couple who now have her. I also feel that within two years of that time, she will have forgotten who she really is and will have learned the language of the new people; she wouldn't know anything different.

To this day I can't get the image of those children out of my mind. I've had no more visions from Madeline, either, and I suppose she went on to communicate with someone else like myself, maybe someone stronger than me who will be able to convince the authorities to listen to them. I feel that if the police were to have looked around the Spanish coastal areas at the time of the abduction, quite possibly near a fishing village, they would have found her. In the meantime, of course, she may have been taken to another place altogether.

༺༻

27ᵗʰ August 2014, *The McCanns and the Conman*
Christine and I watched the documentary, *The McCanns and the Conman* on T.V. this night. It talked about the mysterious disappearance of Madeline McCann, including the setting of the location at the time and the various people involved with the case, and also of those seen in the area who could be considered as a suspect. As I watched, I started getting very strong intuitive feelings of the people I saw.

I believe that the lady, called "Jane" in the documentary, has had a big involvement in Madeline's abduction. I feel she was in the back seat of the car when "George" took her from the man called "Joe". I heard a small girl's voice say, "She did it! She took me away from Mummy and Daddy, and she is blaming another man called George, to save her friend from getting caught!"

I strongly feel that Madeline conveyed the following message to me while I viewed this program;

"She – Jane – wanted me [Madeline] for herself or someone to look after me [Madeline] for her for a while. She [Jane] pretended to be looking for me. She is not to be trusted and is not Mummy's friend!"

༺༻

To this day I have heard nothing from the British police, and Christine has even tried contacting them through a page that specifically says their police are being trained to listen to psychics! She, too, still hasn't gotten a reply. I truly hope they find her and that she gets to be reunited with her real family.

ଚ୍ଚେ

Part III

TRUE Ghost Stories

The next part is of some short stories from people I have read for, who I have asked if they'd be willing to share here with the public.

Each one is of a real, personal experience that is told in his or her own words. Names are true although some people have asked to have a pseudonym instead.

I ask you to respect their views and please enjoy reading their true, ghostly encounters…

A Heavenly Encounter

By Kevin

It would've been the August or December school holidays of 1978, (or there abouts), at the time of this personal experience. For many years I'd kept it to myself, until around sometime in 2005 when I began to mention to a few people what had happened, as not many people would possibly believe that it *had* happened on that particular day, so long ago, when I literally saw a physical person – in daylight – suddenly disappear in the blink of an eye.

Then Mum asked me if I'd mind sharing it here…

It was somewhere around two-thirty in the afternoon when my older brother, Arthur, and I were riding our push bikes up and down the street where we used to live. I was about twelve and Arthur, sixteen. It's worth mentioning that our neighbourhood was usually a quiet one, with nobody else around on this actual occasion. We rode to the end of our driveway, turned left and went up the street.

That's when we both saw a man walking down the street towards our house, but on the opposite side of the road to it. It was rather hard not to notice him…

He was dressed in what we thought was a glossy-red type of dressing gown and he seemed to be wearing sandals, or thongs of some sort (called flip-flops in the U.S.A. and U.K.). He had fairly long, ginger-brown hair, and a full beard and moustache of the same colour. We thought his outfit was a bit weird for that time of year, as it was late spring or early summer and he'd have been too warm in it.

Only about a couple of metres away, at the T-junction of another street, we turned our bikes around to head back down and ride past him again.

But he wasn't there.

Now, there weren't many cars parked on the sides of the road nor were there many trees wide enough for the man to have hidden behind them. And he wouldn't have had time to cross the road to go into the house, either.

So where was he?

He had just vanished!

We rode around for ages afterward, looking for where he might have gone, but we never found him at all – anywhere! Eventually we decided to go back home, feeling a little spooked and we told Mum what we'd just seen.

But as we stood in the front door of our hallway describing him to her, we saw the small figurine of Jesus Christ on a display shelf on the wall behind her.

We'd suddenly realised who we'd seen.

The man walking down the street towards our house in the weird clothes, had looked exactly the same as this little statue!

I had a chill run down my spine. It was incredible! We had actually *seen* Jesus walking down our street, really seen him with my own eyes, in physical form!

This encounter gives me reason to believe that he really does exist. Sadly, I've never seen him again since then (although I'd like to) and even after all of these years I can still remember it as if it was just yesterday that it had happened. I can see the man's face quite clearly in my mind!

ೞಙ

Back in 1997, just before Arthur died, he and I had talked about "*that day*"; we were surprised to know that we both remembered how it went, every little detail! The fact that we'd *both* seen the same man, in the *same* experience – and that he'd *disappeared* from both of us – it was amazing.

Looking back, I feel that we were "blessed" for having had that once-in-a-lifetime experience. It will stay with me for the rest of my life, too.

༄༅

*Mum's actual figurine of
Jesus Christ*

Brush with a Bad Entity

By Belinda

I was twelve years old in 1990 when I had my first spiritual experience.

My best mate at the time, Fiona, had a grandmother who read Tarot cards. I guess you could say that I had always had a keen interest in astrology and in the supernatural world, mostly for the unexplained phenomena that occurs, and also for the ghost-type of experiences we hear about. I had always wanted to have my cards read and one day Fiona arranged for me to have a reading with her grandmother, Helen. I was so excited and couldn't wait to see what my cards were going to reveal.

Of course, I had the typical teenage questions to ask (about my boyfriend, my parents, etc.) but what really interested me the most was the fact that Helen said I had "A Gift".

"What do you mean?" I asked her. "Can you tell me more about it please?"

"You are a naturally spiritual child," she said. "You can sense things that many people can't. In order to use this Gift properly, you need to develop the right skills and learn more about them." She later went on to invite me to her spiritual group that she ran at night once a week in her local community centre nearby. "People come to these groups to learn different types of reading techniques and meditations," she said.

Of course, I really wanted to go to it. I told Mum about my reading and of what Helen had said, and that she thought I should develop this Gift further. Mum was a bit wary about it at first as she didn't know Helen, but most of all she thought I was a bit too young to go. She did let me go in the end, after I was able to get a lift with Fiona's Mum, and the following Monday after school I raced to Fiona's house and quickly got changed.

I was impatient, and time was just going so slowly! We had dinner, spoke for a bit, wasted more time and then finally headed off. We pulled up at the community centre. It was quite dark and I was nervous, because I didn't know what would happen or what might be expected of me.

It turned out not to be that scary after all. Inside, chairs were placed in a circle, all the lights were off but in the centre of the circle was a tray of sand, some crystals and some candles, which gave the room a nice, soft lighting. I was the youngest one there, as everyone else looked to be in their mid-twenties or older. I felt a bit out of place.

We took a seat and settled down for a meditation; Helen always started a spiritual meeting session with one. I had never meditated before and I was hoping that she was going to give us some type of instruction so I didn't look like a complete idiot! Luckily for me, she explained everything in advance.

That night we explored Psychometry, a type of reading of a person's energies from an object belonging to them, usually of personal value. We finished the evening with reading some auras from the members there, and I continued going to these weekly sessions for the next month or so, learning so many new and interesting things, including stuff I'd never heard of before. It was my third week at this spiritual circle that I had my first, totally unexpected, ghostly experience.

We were set up to do an aura reading for one of the group's ladies, named 'Tracie'. She would've been the youngest there until I started coming along; she was probably around twenty-five or so. The candles were lit and placed around her as she sat very still in her chair. The rest of us were approximately three metres away from her, calm and quiet, staring in her direction. Some people softly commented on what they saw with her and others stayed quiet. Although I remember seeing some different colours around her, I was still very shy and didn't want to say something stupid or wrong, so I chose to keep quiet, too.

It was all very quiet for a good five minutes, as though everyone was concentrating quite hard on her. Then out of nowhere, Tracie launched some five feet into the air, clearly in a shocked state. Then I was thrown back by an unseen force. It was like a massive cold rush went through my entire body. Suddenly the centre's doors slammed shut so loudly that we all jumped with fright.

"Are you okay, Belinda?" Helen asked. She and a few others had seen me fly backwards.

"Yes, I think so," I replied, quite shaken. Nothing like this had ever happened to me and neither had I ever seen anything like it in my whole life!

Everyone seemed dazed and shocked as they tried to work out the situation. But Helen was having none of it. She obviously knew what had gone on for she walked straight over to Tracie, who had collected herself from the fall, and she pulled her aside by the arm quite firmly. I think Helen told her to wait until everyone had left so she could speak to her in private, for Tracie stayed there quietly, looking a bit cranky but keeping to herself.

The meeting wrapped up pretty quickly after that. People left in a weird state and when only myself and two other women were left, Helen went up to her. I was still a bit spooked and kept my distance, but I couldn't help hearing parts of their conversation.

"What you have done tonight was totally unacceptable and will *not* be tolerated by any member here!" said

Helen. "You are permanently dismissed from this group and you will no longer be welcome here. Is that understood?"

All I could think was, '*Shit, what the hell did she do that was so wrong for her to be permanently barred?*'.

Tracie protested, trying to wriggle her way out of the dismissal, but Helen stayed firm and the young woman left in a huff.

"Now, Belinda, are you okay?" Helen asked me again.

"Yeah, I'm okay. I just don't understand what happened. What did she do that was so bad?"

"Tracie brought a bad spirit in with her when she arrived," she explained. "But it leapt out of her during the aura reading and went straight through you. That's when you were thrown backwards. And it left through the front doors."

"Is that why they slammed?" I asked, as too many questions swam through my head all at once.

"Yes. It was the evil entity that slammed them shut."

I didn't know what to make of this. Was it real? Did I really get thrown back because of a dark spirit?

"Did she know she'd brought that entity with her?"

"Yes," said Helen, nodding. "I'm sure she'd have to have known it. That's why she should never have sat in the circle."

I only went back to another five or six meetings after that, not because I was scared or because I thought I had learnt everything, but because I felt I had learnt enough to go on my own path of spiritual self-discovery.

༺༻

Nanna and Her Simpatcona

By Christine C

I had always been close to my grandmother (Nanna). We had shared an understanding that there is more than this world, and this bonded us in a unique way. One day, when she was in hospital, she said to me, "Come *Simpatcona* (my Sweet One). I wish to talk to you because no one understands me like you do."

I sat down beside her on her bed and she held my hand.

"I see Angels," she told me. "They are singing the most beautiful songs."

I fought my tears and held her hand tighter.

"That's wonderful, Nanna," I said, assuring her.

She eventually came out of the hospital but at eighty-four years of age, she was not well and slowly declined until she met her passing in 2010. At the funeral I was inconsolable. I could not stop crying and was confused as to why I was so upset, given that I knew she was in a better place.

And then it hit me…

Now, I need to go back in time a little for this to make sense.

A number of years previously, her brother had passed away. I was at the funeral and everyone was hysterical with grief… Except for me. I was sitting in the back row, grinning like a mad person!

Why?

Because I was not seeing what everyone else was seeing. *They* saw a coffin positioned on the stage. But on either side of that coffin *I* saw two huge Angels.

They must have stood about nine feet tall and they glowed with golden-white light. I saw them lift my Uncle from his physical form and take him up to the heavens. I felt so much love and beauty in that experience and I knew he was fine.

Back to Nan's funeral...

Remembering my Uncle's funeral while at Nan's, my sorrow turned to rage.

'*Nanna!*' I screamed in my head. '*How dare you! How dare you not show yourself to me today! Your brother showed himself and he is not even directly of my blood! And you are my Nanna! Show yourself!*' I ordered her.

And in an instant, she was there: sitting in a chair at the front of the chapel, facing everyone, in her purple trousers and indigo T-shirt.

My heart leapt. There she was, looking at everyone, checking out who was there in her strong, silent, observing way. My tears stopped and I was smiling. I knew she was okay and, I got to see her one last time.

My grandmother's birthday was in August and she passed away in November. Fast forward to August the following year and my life was hectic, where I barely had a moment to think. One morning I woke up with a *bang* to the sound of my fire alarm screeching at five a.m. No matter what I did, I could not get it to shut off. After about fifteen minutes battling with it, I got it to stop. Relief! I thought no more of it... until the next morning, when it did exactly the same thing!

Only this time, it *would* stop, then suddenly start again a few moments later, eventually silencing itself. This went on for days, confusing and frustrating me. And then it dawned on me... It was Nanna's birthday.

Suddenly happy, I screamed into space, "Happy Birthday Nanna! Sorry, I forgot. I love you!"

After that, the smoke alarm stopped going off every morning – it was Nanna reminding me that she was still around.

I miss her so much and I regret that we didn't have more time together. I know she is watching me and looking after me from wherever she is. I know this because she is always in my heart.

And I am – and always will be – her *Simpatcona*.

ಬಿಂಛ

---

* Editor's Note: The Christine of this story is not related to the author, (as being the daughter, Christine K. Duncan, of Joyce B Duncan).

Michelle's Nanna

By Michelle

Nanna Janes and I had always had a very close, strong relationship. She was my Dad's mum and at eighty-nine years old, she was moved into a nursing home, where over the years, she eventually got Dementia. Though she began to forget her friends and family, she always remembered me because, I believe, I was always visiting her there. Eventually the time came when she forgot my name but not my face; she was in the third stage of Dementia by then.

Right towards the end of her life, I didn't get to see much of her at all and it was hard on me, because I loved her, but I had a son to look after and a full-time job. Then came the day I was at work, standing at the office photocopier, when all of a sudden, I heard her familiar voice, just like she was standing in the room with me, it was so clear. "Oh Michelle, I'm so tired all the time. I just don't want to be here anymore..."

I wondered if I'd heard right – Nanna was supposed to be in the nursing home. How could I hear her here?

The office was very small and I looked around it, but there was no one else there.

No one knew how close to passing over Nanna Janes was, but it was obviously coming very soon.

"I'm just so tired," I heard Nanna say again. "I don't want to be here anymore, Michelle."

I stopped, knowing I'd seen things like this on television and a quick thought came to my mind.

'*You know what to do,*' I told myself. '*Just answer Nan!*'

So quickly, I did.

"Nan, you're ninety-five years old. You have lived a long, happy life and if you want to go, just go. Go be with your loved ones who are waiting for you, but always remember that I love you, and always will."

After saying that, I felt the atmosphere in the room change; it was very calm, and 'lighter', easier to breathe. Later that night, while relaxing in the lounge room with my partner, I told him what I'd experienced.

"Well, if she was to pass away in the next two to three days," he said, "then what you heard was true."

Straight away I heard:

'*No. She will be here for the next two weeks, but not by the end of the third week.*'

"No," I said to him, repeating the clear message. "Nanna will be here in two weeks, but she won't be here in three."

That was the 6th October 2010.

Just over two weeks later, on Friday 22nd I received a telephone call from one of my Nan's daughters.

"Nanna Janes was taken to hospital about two weeks ago," she said. "She's refused to eat or even drink at the nursing home."

I gasped: this was too close to my message from her.

"She was put on a drip to keep her fluids up," my Aunty went on, "but there's nothing more they can do for her. The doctors say that her time is approaching."

I was affected in a bad way. I hadn't seen her in ages and I wanted to give her a kiss goodbye before she actually went.

Around 21st October Nanna was taken back to the nursing home and my Aunt was informed to gather the family together. After a lengthy conversation with her, she'd asked me not to go visit Nan.

"Remember her for who she was before she got this way," she'd said.

As much as I wanted to go to her, I knew I had said my goodbyes on that Friday in the office. But I really wanted to give her a physical kiss farewell. I was that busy at work and with other commitments that day, so I could not get to the nursing home anyway. Yet she was on my mind all day.

Just after eight the following morning, on Saturday 23rd, my Aunt rang me again to tell me that Nanna had passed away late the night before. This was two weeks and two days from that Friday – more than two weeks but less than three as I had been told from Spirit.

Later on, I asked two spiritually-attuned people, whom I trusted, what had happened, how could I have heard Nan on the Friday, yet she had died two weeks later.

Both told me the reason was that because Nan and I had had a very strong bond, she had chosen to come to me (before passing on) to get my approval to leave this life. She needed the "O.K." to move on.

I told these psychics my story of my Nan and they said that once I gave her the approval to let go, her soul left the body for good and her body shut down. This was the reason she would not eat or even open her mouth for food or drink, as there was nowhere in her body for it to go. Her soul had departed it.

R.I.P. Nanna Janes. I love you.
And always will.
Michelle

Beautiful Spirits

Nana Janes

The Feather at the Footy

By Lisa

My dad, Robert Gilmore, was in a nursing home because of dementia and recovering from an operation to remove a tumour that was discovered from a sore found on his head, which developed from him repeatedly beating it against the wall; cancer was behind it.

My niece, Melissa, and I were particularly close to Dad. In April 2011 we went to the football on the Friday night to watch the Bulldogs verse Parramatta at Homebush stadium, a large area that can seat thousands of people. She was about thirteen years old then.

We were in the unreserved seating area in front of the goals. Just before the game started, a white feather (about 3-4 inches long) drifted down from the sky, falling onto the field in front of us about fifteen metres away.

Watching it fall, I knew it carried symbolic importance because for one, there were no birds in sight. So where did it come from?

"Oh look at that! A feather!" I said to Melissa, "What are the chances of that – it's night time!"

She saw it falling too.

"It means something," I said, having no idea what was to come, "like... it's spiritual, or an angel... or something – it's an eerie feeling though, isn't it?"

"Yeah," she said, really caught by the moment.

Next morning between nine to nine-thirty, the nursing home called Mum. We were both there with her when the call came. It wasn't good.

"Your father's collapsed and they've called an ambulance," she said calmly.

I had to stop for a minute, because it seemed she was oblivious to how severe the situation was.

"But hang on," I said, "They've called an ambulance. It's serious!"

"Well, that's what they said, Love. I don't know what's wrong with him. They didn't say!"

I wasn't wasting time on it.

"Come on, get dressed," I said to Melissa, and to Mum, I said, "Come on, we're going to the nursing home!"

We left as soon as we could, with me driving and trying not to lose it.

At the home, I went straight for Dad's room, but on the way there we met a nurse who recognised us.

"How's Dad," I asked her.

"Sorry, he's gone," she said, softly.

It didn't make sense; this isn't what I came here to hear. "No! I've come to see Dad," I explained, as if she didn't get my meaning.

"Sorry… he's gone," she said, and she covered her mouth with her hands, as if she was sad.

"Where is he?" I asked, still refusing to accept the news.

"In his room," she said.

"Thanks," I said, but couldn't stand to wait any longer.

Forcing myself to hold it together, I went straight to Dad's ward, with Mum and Melissa tagging along.

The curtain was pulled right around his bed and everything seemed cold and quiet – awfully quiet. I knew now, without a doubt, that Dad was dead. My heart raced as I walked into the room. I clenched my jaws and I went up to the curtain to open it, then suddenly I remembered

Melissa – his granddaughter – was right there beside me. Would she handle seeing him?

"Are you sure you want to see this?" I asked her.

"Yes," she said.

"Are you *sure*?" I was worried that she wasn't really prepared to see her Pop's body; she was so young.

"Yes," she said again, bravely, too.

I could see she was alright about it and gently went ahead.

Quietly I pulled the curtain open. There was Dad – my wonderful Dad – laying peacefully in the bed. It hurt like hell to know he'd really died. He was only sixty-seven and I know age will get us in the end if we don't die before that, but still, I wanted to cry and tell him how much I loved him.

It wasn't until this moment that something clicked.

I looked at Melissa, with a slight grin.

She looked at me, too – she was thinking the same thing

"The feather," we softly said at the same time. Our smiles lightened the mood.

"Now we know what it meant," I said.

"Yep, now we know."

"Know what?" Mum asked. "What feather?"

We told her what had happened to us the night before.

"Well," she said, sort of smiling, "I guess he'd come to tell you he was going!"

That's exactly what we thought, too. He was somehow letting us know that his time was up and he was about to go. I'm so grateful he did that. It meant so much.

It still does.

We love you Dad, and we miss you still.

༺༻

Beautiful Spirits

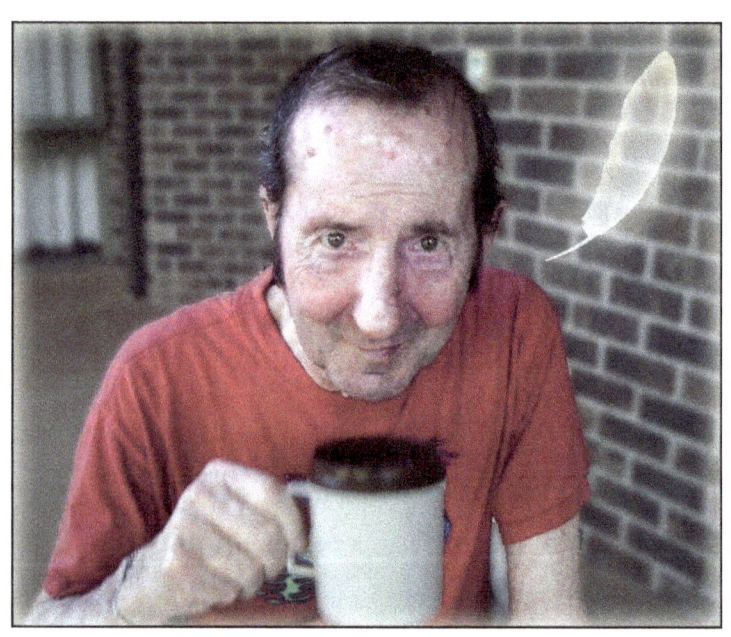

My Dad, Robert

Meet Me at the Races
By Dave

I start my story with a bit of a problem. I enjoyed Joyce's first book and it reminded me of some interesting experiences I'd had when I'd lived in a previous house around fifteen years ago. It had 'unexplained' issues in it. So when Joyce asked me if I'd like to include a story in this second book, I knew what I could say, but I had no real idea how to put it into words. Would it have impact? Meaning? Might it be actually considered as a story worth listening to? Well, hopefully this one is…

I once had a best friend called Steve, who was a top motor sport racer for easily a decade or so. I worked with him as his photographer and cameraman for many years. Most of our racing was in Perth, W.A. although we also travelled around Australia to other racetrack comps. It was a great experience, but in 2015 I stopped going to race meetings because things became politically problematic within the industry.

Steve continued racing when he could, though his health had been deteriorating over a couple of years. I knew he had been severely ill for some time, though I didn't know he was dying; he'd kept his condition a secret from all but his family. I still believe I had found out only by accident! He was so effective at hiding his pain in those final days that his passing, in the beginning of March, caught everyone out.

I was fortunate that I had a beautiful partner, 'Sam' who gave me much-needed mental strength in getting through those difficult days, as I had become numb to everything around me. She helped me keep perspective and just after his death, I made the last 2015/2016 meeting of the season, where his car was on display one last time.

But it just wasn't the same without him. His larger-than-life presence cut a massive absence in the crowds. His distinctive laugh – so big, so full and deep – was silent. My heart went completely out the window being there and, filled with pain, my world descended on me like a ton of bricks. I was convinced that the racing scene could go on without me being a part of it. Steve had made such a huge difference to my life that now, I was totally lost. I felt directionless and no matter how much I tried to enjoy my photography, the enthusiasm and passion was gone, along with my best mate.

November came and I woke up for another working day beside Sam, still trying to come to terms with Steve's passing. Usually Sam stirs not long after me, but this morning she was still asleep, when the most unusual thing happened. Interestingly, Sam has the ability to sense energies and to see spirits. Sometimes she can be a bit scared about it, and how they can easily communicate with her if they want to.

She mumbled something as I started to get dressed. To me, this meant she'd woken.

"What did you say, Hun?" I asked.

She mumbled again.

'Blimey,' I thought, continuing to change, *'she's hard to rouse this morning!'*

"Honey, could you please repeat that?" I asked her nicely. "I couldn't quite catch what you said."

"Uurrr… write down, "Meet me at the races"," she replied in a low, lethargic drawl.

'Ah! I've figured out what this is all about!' I thought, turning to her. "You're talking in your sleep, aren't you?"

We both do this, often with hilarious stories to share between us afterward. I went to the bathroom, content in thinking her comment was simply an extension of her dream. She was awake by the time I returned.

"I know what you were saying now," I said as I entered the room. "It was part of a dream, wasn't it?"

"What was?"

"Well, y'know – what you said just now. Was it to do with a dream?"

"I didn't say anything," she replied, her face straight; she was serious, she really didn't think she'd said a word.

'Okay...' I thought to myself. *'A bit of a mystery. I'll ask later on, but right now I've gotta get to work.'*

Nine hours of moving boxes in a stuffy room went by then I was back home, very keen to know more.

"So what happened this morning?" I began, once we'd found some quiet time together. "You mumbled twice. Both times I asked you to repeat yourself. Then you said, "Meet me at the races." Yet you reckon you didn't say anything?"

This time, something seemed to spark in her head.

"Oh yeah, I remember seeing someone," she replied. "He distinctly said that just before I woke up."

"He? That's intriguing. Umm... what did he look like?"

She described Steve perfectly; sure enough, it was him. Now, typically, I would have dismissed the whole thing as a projection of her mind – that's what dreams are, right? But somehow it felt unusual that she would see Steve in her sleep and more, that he'd said to meet him at the races. Funnily enough, tomorrow just so happened to be a race weekend, too. Maybe it really was a message I was supposed to hear? Curiosity got the better of me.

Race day arrived and we drove down to the track. We'd barely gone through the main gates and Sam felt the energies...

Intense energies.

But they disappeared just as suddenly, apparently, and despite Sam feeling very uneasy, I encouraged her to come with me to the pits, where I'd catch up with people I had met back in the day. Afterward we'd go up to the stand to watch the racing.

She agreed and we spent a couple of hours wandering around. I found being at the races invigorated me. It was great meeting old friends, seeing the cars in action, smelling the high-octane fuel; I wanted to get my camera rolling just as I used to do. Eventually we went up to the stand for a good view of the track. About ten minutes later, Sam 'had company'.

"He's here," she said simply.

Ahh, the moment had come.

"Sooo..." I began, attempting to sound casual, "whereabouts is he?"

"Just behind us. Leaning on a fence."

Just to re-emphasise, I genuinely have no gift of seeing spirits. I'm literally relying on critical thinking and logic. But for the life of me, logic was literally not answering anything for me!

And despite knowing I wouldn't see him, I looked along the fence anyway – coolly, as if I wasn't looking at something that wasn't there. Did I expect to see a bend in the wire? Would Steve's outline show in it and thus prove his after-life existence?

"So, we got the message," I said. I also don't believe in stuffing around; let's just get to the gist of why we were here. "What does he want me to do?"

Sam nodded and continued her gaze of the grounds, apparently taking in what the energies were telling her. Then she got it.

"He seems to say that you should continue to return here; watch the racing. You've missed being here… at the end of the day…"

And there it was. Steve's message for me.

It was as if someone had just opened the curtain and let a brighter day shine in. He was right, of course. I'd enjoyed watching the racing, and seeing the people who'd come to watch it, too. Also being among the pit-boys, who's faces were always fixed on the job at hand. And I loved filming the action, capturing the wildness of metal in full speed! Sam also, was caught up in the excitement of the races. Now I knew what I had to do.

I had my sense of direction back, my purpose.

When the last race was done we said our goodbyes to the gang in the pits and left for our car. Just as we approached the main exit, Sam stopped, looking less certain, almost disturbed. She was sensing something again, but was it another message from Steve?

"I feel an energy again…" she said anxiously. "This one's not him, it's… different." She had that far-away stare that says she's 'tuning in'. "Somewhat shapeless?" she suggested to herself. "Seems angry. Very angry."

Now that wasn't expected; not for me, anyhow.

"It's definitely the feeling of someone, or something else," she went on. "But it's unidentifiable."

"This might not be an easy one to answer," I said, concerned. "And I don't fancy hanging around to find out."

I could see she was feeling drained and tired from her sensory work of earlier, something she'd been doing for most of the day, in fact. We got to the car and drove home, though I still had some questions that needed answering. Hearing from Steve merely scratched the surface of a whole new experience for me, and I was enthusiastic to resolve it. When she was ready, I asked.

"Have you sensed Steve before?"

"In truth…" she cautiously began, "a few times before, yes."

This was exciting; I wanted to know more. It seems that for Sam, Steve had been communicating with her nearly immediately.

"One particular memory of him is of that special day, when the hearse did a lap of honour for him before the funeral," she said. "Steve's spirit stood behind it as it set off down the track, watching it make that "one last lap." He was smiling, and he felt so proud and happy that he was loved by so many people."

Not only that, it seemed he'd also made an appearance or two at our apartment (which we'd bought after he'd died). It was during a tough financial episode in which I'd lost hope of surviving, when I'd felt a never-ending sense of disappointment in myself of failure.

"Why did he make an appearance then?" I asked, curious. "Did he say something?"

"He relayed a message to me, to tell you to never give up." Sam briefed me of the time and of how things did seem to genuinely improve after that. Those darker days where home was an impending loss and working hard to pay the bills, passed, becoming less of a struggle for us both.

All of this news came to me like a flood of understanding. It seems that 'someone' had been keeping an eye on us when we needed him. That's the sort of man he was. In life, he was very devout in his religion, with upstanding morals and a strong sense of family to everyone. So here he'd been, working away in the background to keep us stable, and me grounded, via Sam.

ಐಞ

Nowadays I know more about Sam's abilities and I accept them as 'normal' for her. She's comfortable when Steve 'drops by' for a visit (which he does now and again), though it wasn't always the case with the presence of some spirits…

A "young" male once followed her around for an hour, continuously singing, *"Call me maybe"*. It drove her nuts, and I can see how that sort of thing can be annoying. She got so fed up with him that she swung round, threatening to send him down to the pits of Hell. The spirit shut up then and promptly buggered off. Sam can be scary like that. The spirit did a wise thing.

Sam says that I have the same sort of abilities as her, that we all do, and though I'm not sceptical of spiritual happenings, I'm still unsure about whether *I* can do what she does. It's not something I'm rushing into. But who knows?

One day, I will meet him at the races…

ಐಂಬ

Car Racetrack

Bobbie's Bookmark

I will close with the time I had had an interesting experience with a lady named Bobbie, for my readings will not end but just keep getting stronger, and I will be writing these stories for many years to come at this rate!

At the Broadmeadow Railway Exhibition in mid-August of 2014, my plans had been a little different to normal. I usually have a small train layout with me at this event but due to illness in the family, I didn't take it this time. But as it worked out, Spirit knew I would be rushed off my feet and wouldn't be able to watch not only my model trains from little fingers wanting to touch it, but also from keeping an eye on the craft and giftware Christine and I were selling (clever spirits). It turned out to be a very busy weekend.

I sold six copies of my book, one of which went to a lady called Vicki, who was excited after reading the back cover and decided to buy one. I give a complimentary bookmark with each copy and seeing it, she asked if I could give her two more for her two friends, for she knew they would love my book too.

"And would you mind signing them too?" she asked.

"Yes, of course I can," I replied, asking her for their names.

"One's Bobbie," she said up first.

We chatted for quite a while as I wrote on the bookmarks.

"Do you give private readings? she asked.

"I do, but as we're not local to your area, my daughter and I can give you a group reading. We recommend you get some friends together and we can make a day trip down to read for you all."

"Oh really? That's great! And I've got a few friends I could probably get to come over for it!"

"Well it usually works in well for us all, as Christine can read for some of your guests and I can read for the others, so instead of it taking say, six hours for six people, it will only take three hours between us."

She thought this was fantastic, especially as the price was the same with whoever did the readings.

"How do I contact you then when I'm ready?" she checked.

I gave her a brochure we'd made that covered all the information she'd need, including prices, times and contacts. She was thrilled and eager to organise a group booking as soon as she could.

It turned out that, not only did I make her friends very happy with their bookmarks, but Bobbie was so excited with a particular part of hers. I didn't realise when I had signed it just *how* my writing had appeared on it.

Two weeks after that weekend event, I received a couple of text messages from her:

> "Hi Joyce this is Bobbie. I'm a good friend of Vicki, who you met at the train expo a couple of weeks ago. Vicki gave me your book to read and I couldn't put it down. I just wanted to say thank you for sharing your story with us and thank you for signing a bookmark for me."

In brackets was...

> "in my Nanna's handwriting, mind you. I'd love to meet you one day in person."

In the short-worded style of text messaging, I replied:

"Thank you. No problems. Would love to meet you and I'm sure your Nanna will help you get a group together when the time is right. Just have faith."

That evening I was amazed at what Bobbie had said about her Nanna's writing. I was grateful to her Nanna for having been with me when signing the bookmark, even though I wasn't aware of it! And it sure meant a lot to Bobbie.

As I was thinking about our possible meeting someday, I got the distinct feeling that someone in spirit was with me. Then I saw the vision of a small brown dog which appeared to be resting its head on a lady's right thigh. Beyond the knee was a lounge or sofa, with reddish or brown coverings. Then the lady appeared in full, stroking the little dog. She was of average height, with grey hair and an elderly face. At first I thought it was my imagination running away with me – it so happened to be a 'Nanna', when I was thinking of Bobbie and her Nanna – so I dismissed it.

A couple of hours passed and while preparing for bed, I still had this image hovering around. I was frustrated and didn't know what to do, but I settled down for the night anyway, hoping to sleep well.

The next morning, I awoke with the awful feeling of being in trouble for not having contacted Bobbie about my vision of the lady with the dog. It persisted through breakfast, too. So I decided to text her again.

"Hi Bobbie, this is Joyce. Sorry for being a nuisance, but did you have a small brown dog that passed away, or do you have one still with you? And is Mum still with you?"

I asked about her mother because I also sensed that she had gone over too. But in case I was wrong, I didn't want to alarm her with bad news. A couple of hours passed when her reply came through.

> "Sorry, I was in a circle meditating when I got your message. Mum had a small brown dog before she passed away years ago, then I inherited the dog until it passed over a few years later."

This blew me away, for I had never known or seen this lady. I was ecstatic. I felt that my spirit guide, Lydia, was definitely with me, and that my gifts have finally been returned, as promised in my first book.

When finally speaking with her on the phone, I explained to Bobbie my vision of the little dog and the lady.

"I can see your Nanna with you, too," I said. "Were you closer to your Nan more than your Mum? Your Mum said that she is with the grandchildren more than you. And I can see your Nan giving you a big hug."

"Yes!" she cried. "Nan was always there for me when Mum wasn't, and Mum wasn't a cuddly person."

As the conversation went on I felt that Bobbie was a little stressed.

"Are you tired? Or have you been a bit stressed lately?" I asked.

"Yes! We have to move and I don't know where we will go," she replied.

"Nan is showing me a long caravan. Maybe you will have to live in a caravan until you find your new home?"

"Oh no, I don't want to live in a caravan!" she blurted out. "There's a caravan park at the end of our street. Maybe it means we will be living near it and I'll be able to look out of the windows and see them?"

I didn't quite think this was so. "That's possible, but I feel you may still live in one temporarily for a couple of weeks until your home is ready to move in to."

I was feeling stronger and stronger in my psychic abilities and I sensed that I have met Bobbie before, somewhere, sometime, maybe in the past.

When our conversation finally came to an end I didn't want to hang up, but time was against me, for I needed to prepare my family's next meal.

"Okay, so when the time is right, we will meet up," I said, "and I feel that I will be doing a reading for you, too."

Within minutes of us hanging up, Bobbie had sent through a message with a photograph included. The picture showed an elderly lady giving a woman of around twenty a big hug, her right arm around the younger one's shoulders, just as I had seen in the vision. The text said:

"Nana and me."

The next day around noon I received another text from Bobbie:

"Guess what? My husband just told me that when he was around five or six, he lived in the caravan park at the end of this street in between house moves, until his father passed away. And it was a long van as well!"

I was over the moon.

༺༻

Beautiful Spirits

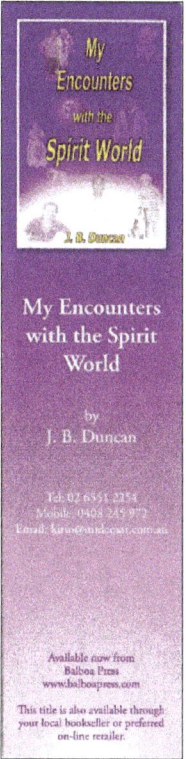

*Bookmark for My Encounters with
the Spirit World*

So now I feel my readers know enough of me and my Gifts. I hope that I have helped others in some small way just by sharing my experiences with you all. If anyone needs me, or my daughter's, help, please feel welcome to contact us.

I leave you with the following meditation, hoping you will find what you seek with it.

୫୬ଓଃ

A Meditation into the Spirit World

This easy meditation will help you to visit your loved ones.

Before you start the meditation, make sure the mobile phone is turned off (and if you have a landline phone, take it off the hook). The television and radio should also be off, although if you like to have music playing at this time, choose music that is soft and flowing, and have the volume low.

First, find a comfortable chair to relax in, with your feet on the floor. If you prefer to sit on the floor, find a soft cushion and place it where you may feel at ease and take a Lotus position (if possible). Place your hands on your knees with palms upwards. Close your eyes and clear your mind of thoughts and worries.

Imagine you are sitting in a bubble. Ask your guides or angels for protection while on this journey. Take a deep breath and imagine that with every breath you draw in, your bubble fills with soft, white light. Then exhale all the negative energy. Repeat this for as long as needed, filling your bubble with the white light each time you inhale and release any negative thoughts and feelings each time you breath out. When your bubble is full of the light, relax (breathing comfortably), and watch the light gently swirling around you.

See the light turn from white into gold and allow it to absorb into your body. Feel yourself being transported through a portal to a beautiful forest scene, surrounded by pleasant trees and scented flowers. Take the time to smell their perfume, to feel the breeze and appreciate the safe, calm setting.

Looking around, you see a bush track leading off into the distance. Walk towards it, follow its path to where a cottage, hut or cave appears. It, too, is pleasant to see and is safe to enter. Feel yourself being drawn to it, going through its entrance. Your golden light helps to illuminate the new surroundings inside this place.

If you are here to make contact with a departed loved one, then allow for that person, or pet, to be there. Do not *expect* a specific someone, for she or he may be unable to appear in this particular visit; just allow for anyone of those in Spirit to make themselves present to you. They will greet you warmly and be ready to communicate with you.

Talk with them, mentally send them your thoughts and they will reply in the same way. Don't be afraid to share your feelings with them, or to ask them questions. If you have a problem that needs addressing, ask them to help you with how to solve it. If you, (or someone you know) is sick, or fighting an illness, ask this spirit loved one for healing energy to restore your health, (or the health of someone you are asking for).

If you are here to make contact with a spirit guide or guardian angel, again, allow the guide(s) or angel(s) to be there according to how they present themselves to you. Sometimes they may appear in a different form to what you may have expected – it will be relevant to your needs and personal situation at that time of your life.

Simply *allow* the scene to unfold naturally, without controlling who or what must be included, or how or why certain things must occur. If a specific individual doesn't appear, don't worry nor be angry, for *you*, too, must be at an emotional and mental level that is ready to see them. Sometimes our emotions get in the way of things and can override the 'delicate' link of these connections.

There will always be another chance, another meditation, later on.

To be successful – or to feel confident – in these experiences, try to make a regular meditation on the same day and time each week. Spirit will learn of your wishes and sense your efforts and they will know to come to you with this sort of repetition. The link becomes stronger with practice.

Always be grateful for what you receive. Express your thanks and be free with your feelings of love. Above all, be *honest* within yourself in the way you feel, act, or think with this person, pet, guide or angel, for they will already be able to sense your true feelings, they will know what you're thinking. If you are insincere with yourself during the experience, you will, unfortunately, come away from it with uncertainty, perhaps doubting that what you saw or sensed was only imagination. But with genuine care and attention, you will learn to determine when spiritual communication has occurred over any fanciful imaginings.

When you are ready to leave, thank your loved ones and return to the entrance of the cottage, hut or cave. Follow the path through the forest to the place you first arrived, 'see' the portal of light and allow yourself to be drawn through it back to your earthly surroundings.

Become aware of your breathing again, letting the golden light turn to white with each breath in, and release this white light gently through the top of your bubble with each breath out. When the bubble is empty, thank your guides and angels for their protection and allow for your bubble to disappear. Then bring your focus fully into your home surroundings.

You should now feel very relaxed and fully awake.

༺༻

Beautiful Spirits

*Red and yellow roses for
love and peace*

*...from Spirit,
and I*

About the Author

Joyce B. Duncan was born in 1940 in Sunderland, England. She emigrated with her family in January 1951 to Warragamba, N.S.W. Australia.

She had her first apparition in December 1951, aged 11. Since then she's had premonitions and around the age of thirty, she learned to read plain deck cards with her Aunty May. This led to her attending the now closed, Parramatta Spiritual Church through the 1970's, where she learned to tune in to the Spirit World and hone her Gifts of seeing and hearing people who have passed over.

In 1984, her late son, Arthur, asked her to give these gifts away because, in his words, "it was evil". So, in being loyal to him, she did, but she had also asked Spirit to, "please come back if ever I needed you".

She later found out that Arthur had been told by people of the local Churches that what she did was evil.

Then in 2006 her spirit friends came back into her life, telling her to write a book about her spiritual experiences. This was *My Encounters with the Spirit World*. She was told by a medium in 2012 that she would be writing a second book about the return of her spiritual gifts, which forms *Beautiful Spirits*.

It is her fervent wish to share her gifts with everyone with these books, and hope her readers all enjoy, and draw comfort, from them.

"I now know we are all watched over by angels and they give us their love when we need it."
~ Joyce B. Duncan

www.ingramcontent.com/pod-product-compliance
Lightning Source LLC
Chambersburg PA
CBHW050631300426
44112CB00012B/1746